COMMUNICATION CAMPAIGNING

PRIMER FOR SENIOR LEADERS
1ST EDITION

TOM GALVIN

FOREWORD BY MARI K. EDER

DEPARTMENT OF COMMAND, LEADERSHIP, AND MANAGEMENT
SCHOOL OF STRATEGIC LANDPOWER
U.S. ARMY WAR COLLEGE, CARLISLE PA

Table of Contents

List of Figures

List of Tables

Acknowledgements

This Primer was the result of five years of engagement with a lot of people, all trying to make sense of this mysterious 'thing' called strategic communication. I did not set out initially to develop a methodology, rather it became apparent that one was needed—one that looked inside the organization as much as outside. This insight came courtesy of the students of the Senior Leader Communication (later Organizational Communication) elective in the U.S. Army War College resident program. Their interest in the topic and engagement during class inspired me to pursue a methodology in the form of a teachable and flexible thought process rather than a mechanistic model, which I came to view as an unsuitable approach in practice. So, I first thank my students for helping me make this monograph a reality.

My elective co-instructors provided invaluable insights and feedback throughout, and I thank them as well -- Col Lance Clark, U.S. Air Force; COL Dale Watson, U.S. Army; and COL Maurice Sipos, U.S. Army. Dale Watson deserves additional credit for helping shape the six-question approach, which became the basis for a faculty paper used in the core Strategic Leadership course of the resident program beginning in 2017. I also thank U.S. Army War College Professor Charles D. "Chuck" Allen for his feedback on the earliest drafts of my papers that ultimately led to this Primer.

I also thank the Department Chairs during this period—COL Mik McCrea, COL Bobby Mundell, and COL Dale Watson—along with the Department electives coordinator Professor Doug "Muddy" Waters for their support in establishing and sustaining interest in senior leader communication. I also thank the Department's educational technicians—Chiquita Morrison and Genny Hobson—for their support to the elective and for their sharp eyes on the final version of this Primer.

FOREWORD

Major General (Ret.) Mari K. Eder

Strategic communication is both an art and a science, a malleable hybrid process that makes achieving consensus on the best organizational approach to a communications campaign difficult to achieve. Too often, national and military leaders favor the science, and deliver messages that are rational in their construction but uninspiring to stakeholders and members of the organization alike. But too much artistry is also a problem. If the message is not grounded in the identity of the organization, it fails to be authentic or motivating. To this point, there has been little that guides leaders how to integrate the art and science into campaign development. This primer points the way, to mastering the science so that the art can then be applied with a judicious and skillful hand.

Too many senior leaders may think they know how the system works and how to work the system. What do these senior leaders get wrong about strategic communication? First, they rely heavily on their operational experience. Gut instinct has worked before; plus, they believe in their own infallibility. These are the ones who ultimately fail.

Strategic leaders must be fully self-aware of how every aspect of their leadership style, vision, and approach builds a communications platform that either supports their intent or unintentionally undermines it. Approach this primer openly and with a genuine focus on learning that which goes beyond directive, one-way messaging. Strategic communication is different. It is long-term, overarching, and encompasses identity, building coherent narratives and rests on individual and organizational reputation. It is too important to leave to instinct, habit or even past experience alone.

Communication disasters are leadership failures and ultimately can result in campaign failures. Ask General George Patton, a WWII commander who wanted to be known for his audacity on the battlefield, not his words. Both nearly derailed his career. In a famous wartime incident, he was visiting a hospital when he became infuriated at the demeanor of a shell-chocked soldier and slapped him. Then he threatened another, "I should shoot you myself."

Theater commander General Dwight Eisenhower issued a strong public rebuke to Patton and there was extensive negative media fallout from his actions. Even benched, Patton refused to learn from his mistakes. While a consummate operator and troop leader, he had a history of creating public debacles, from speaking out about postwar roles for the U.S. and Britain that was both impulsive and not in line with U.S. campaign objectives to making statements that contradicted his boss. And, following the war, he expressed his disdain for denazification. Hubris ultimately cost him his command. Eisenhower had finally had enough.

Dwight Eisenhower was a masterful communicator who strategically developed and built support for his vision, his goals, and his campaigns. His boss, General George C. Marshall, Chief of Staff of the Army, was likewise a skilled strategic leader. Both of these men succeeded in communicating campaign strategies while building internal and external support despite public pressures, political disruptions, the stress of combat leadership, the wavering support of allies, and other complex distractions - because they steadfastly maintained values consistent with their Army's identity and reputation (both organizational and personal), were consistent in the tone and timing of their narratives, and stayed true to their stated intent. Unlike Patton, they applied large doses of selflessness to their leadership style and kept their personal desires and opinions out of the decision-making process. Country first.

Throughout their long careers, both senior leaders mastered the requirement for patience in achieving their goals, thoroughly undertook all aspects campaign operations planning, practiced the science of leadership and then applied the art of strategic communication. They knew what it took. Eisenhower once said, "I'll tell you what leadership is: its persuasion, and conciliation, and education, and patience. It's long, slow, tough work."

Strategic communication is likewise long, slow, tough work, accomplished in a dynamic and competitive environment of constant scrutiny, criticism, and feedback. But it can succeed.

Success has a better chance when leaders recognize their own foibles, personal blind spots, and inherent tendencies to judge or even pre-judge. In tempering temperament, strategic leaders can communicate with a greater degree of both openness and understanding, and guide their organizations to speak and act as one.

MG Mari K. Eder, USA Ret
Author of
Leading the Narrative: The Case for Strategic Communication

PREFACE. WHY A COMMUNICATION CAMPAIGNING METHODOLOGY?

For ten years, I served as special assistant to various commanders of service component, joint, and combined commands. For five of those years, I led Commander's Action Groups (CAG), designated teams of special assistants who reported directly to a commander.[1] Those assignments were tremendously rewarding and allowed me to see first-hand how several general officers and civilians perceived their environment, engaged with stakeholders, made decisions, formulated and communicated their vision, and ultimately accomplished their missions. It was eye-opening how differently each commander operated, including the degrees to which work at the senior levels got done through informal means – for instance, through collaboration and negotiation – rather than formally through the military bureaucracy.

WHITHER "STRATEGIC" COMMUNICATION?

It also exposed me to how *organizations* communicate ... or not. Throughout my tenures in these organizations, commanders emphasized the need to speak with one voice and act in unison to achieve desired effects. To be sure, each commander was individually a strong communicator and championed his or her own message. But the organization did not always follow along. Even within the same organization with the same commander, some messages resonated yet others did not. For those that resonated, the organization eagerly disseminated the messages through words and deeds as though they owned it. For those that did not, the organization would equivocate, waffle, debate, resist, and so on. Half-hearted words to stakeholders and half-hearted actions followed.

At the same time, there was a lot of churn going on about strategic communication (SC). The Department of Defense's Science Board studied it because of problems arising from the

---

[1] Also known as commander's "initiatives groups" (CIGs), "special studies group" (CSSGs), or "special assistants group" (SAGs). I discuss the roles and responsibilities in Thomas P. Galvin, "Assignment: Special Assistant to the Commander," *Military Review* 95, no. 2 (March-April 2015): 33-38.

Global War on Terror, as it was then known. Teams sponsored by the services, joint community, and NATO made field visits, conducted training sessions, and left behind reams of presentations and documents talking about SC's importance. At the time it was clear that many people had an idea of what good SC looked like, but they could only describe it in terms of what individuals did — speak clearly, show empathy, tailor messages to audiences, and so on. But none could explain in a general sense how to do it from an organization's perspective beyond stressing the importance of synchronizing the messages.[2]

I had the privilege of participating in multiple organization-level communication efforts, including two that were demonstrably successful. One was the Multi-Year Roadmap initiative in Stabilization-Force Bosnia (SFOR) in 2000-2001, when the military commander faced a lack of unity among the civilian agencies implementing the Dayton Accords. The other was the controversial formation of the U.S. Africa Command (AFRICOM). Both changed the strategic environments favorable to the desires of the commanders. Both also saw the respective organizations speaking and acting in unison fully aligned with the commanders' messages with only minimal oversight required from the leadership.[3]

Comparing these success with other less-successful efforts in which I participated, I drew two conclusions. First, too much of the talk on SC was on quick solutions for complex problems. It promised effects on the cheap, which proved impossible to deliver in practice. While the commanders appreciated the long time it took to influence actors in the environment, there were internal or external pressures to change minds quickly. Of course, this was unrealistic, but patience can sometimes be limited at the strategic level. However, my experiences showed that patience is often necessary to achieve lasting effects. The effort at SFOR took many months, while AFRICOM took years of sustained energy to

---

[2] A more thorough history of *strategic communication* in the Department of Defense is provided in Mari K. Eder, *Leading the Narrative: The Case for Strategic Communication* (Annapolis, MD: Naval Institute Press, 2011), 19-44.

[3] Thomas P. Galvin, *Two Case Studies of Successful Communication Campaigns* (Carlisle, PA: U.S. Army War College Press, in press).

bring about the desired effects and change the minds of stakeholders the environments. There were no quick solutions.

The second conclusion was the need to figure out what SFOR, AFRICOM, and other commands who conducted successful communication efforts actually did. Perhaps there were insights that other commanders might find useful. One such insight was that SC as practiced was not sufficient in the general case.

COMMUNICATION AND CHANGE

Another motivation for this Primer is the nexus of change and communication, and in particular how communication failure assures change failure. This has been articulated by many authors, but a fascinating treatment of it is in Paul Gibbons' book *The Science of Successful Organizational Change*,[4] where he discusses the differences between change management and change leadership. In the former, the work of change is outsourced to members or consultants and treated as an external process separate from the mainstream of activity. Change leadership means that the organizational leaders have instituted change as a 'normal' activity. Not surprisingly, Gibbons explains that change management leaders to poorer communication, increasingly the likelihood to failure. Other authors like John Kotter likewise attribute change failure to poor communication.

But, in my experience, military organizations explain things very well. Leaders generally do a good job at presenting the intended change message, and two-way communication is encouraged. When properly employed, the noncommissioned officer chain of support often fills in gaps. Communications channels vertically through the chain of command and horizontally among communities of practice and peer organizations are fairly strong despite silo'ing that can occur in large complex organizations.

I found that there is not consistency between successful change and successful communication. In fact, most change efforts I have witnessed see success in one but failure in the other.

---

[4] Paul Gibbons, *The Science of Successful Organizational Change* (New York: Pearson, 2015), 30-31.

I have personally witnessed plenty of times where communicating the change was done well, in that the leadership did everything reasonably possible to disseminate the change vision and plan, and the members did receive it and showed indications that they understood it sufficiently. But when the change effort failed, blame fell on *poor communication*. In fact, a charge of communication failure is often a proxy for something else wrong with the organization — something no one may be able to put a finger on.[5]

Oddly enough, I have also witnessed times when the change effort succeeded despite being poorly communicated. These included instances when: (1) the impetus was so compelling that the organization made things happen despite a lack of understanding of what they were doing (i.e., doing anything was better than nothing, and the organization sometimes got lucky); (2) the organization was completely beholden to an external process and therefore did not require understanding of what the change was about; or (3) the change effort was pushed through by the guiding coalition alone, somewhat isolated from the rest of the organization.

Certainly all change efforts have a communication component; but the idea change and communication were so closely coupled struck me as wrong. Instead, I believe that although interrelated, the change effort and its associated communication effort are actually distinct and operate on different phasing. The following story is constructed from my various experiences in change and communication, and is graphically displayed in Figure 1.

The story begins with the formulation of an idea in the leader's mind. Note that it is only being formulated, it has yet to take shape, and so the leader is likely socializing the idea with an inner circle of close advisors, key staff leaders, and trusted agents. These individuals are normally expected to keep their conversations with the leader in confidence. Thus, the leader has

---

[5] Art Markman, "'Poor Communication' is Often a Symptom of a Different Problem," *Harvard Business Review* 100, no. 2 (February 2017).

a chance to mature the idea (or abandon it) before socializing it wider.

Leader's Communication Effort	*Organization's Change Effort*

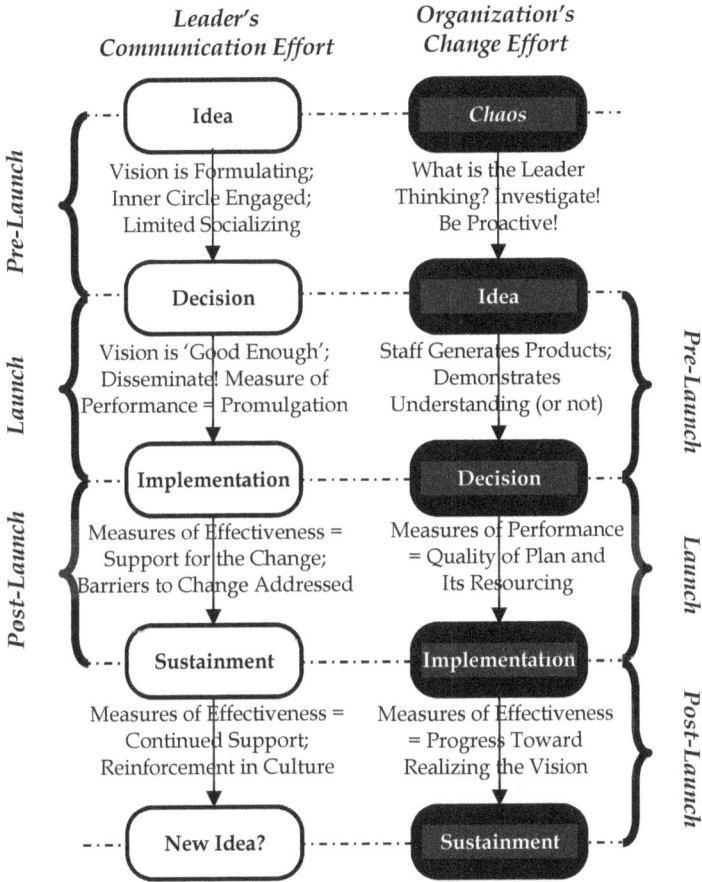

Figure 1. Communication and Change Efforts[6]

Meanwhile, organizational members typically perceive clues that the leader is formulating some sort of idea (of what, they may not know) and begin jockeying for inside information. At its worst, the organization falls into a state of chaos as members leverage contacts among the leader's personal staff for inside information, read into whatever leader communications they can

---

[6] Original graphic developed by author.

access, or take premature action.[7] If the leader's idea was based on something a member said or briefed, everyone is looking for those slides or notes or are cornering the member. Partial truths and mistruths send the organization down rabbit-holes or making bad assumptions. At its worst, it is *chaos*. One can presume that this churn is a partial source of alleged poor communication.

In the next phase, the leader has essentially made up his or her mind about the need for change. The vision is essentially formulated, and the leader signals readiness to engage on it. The leader's decision is essentially made at this point. While the vision may see incremental changes thereafter, transformational change is much more difficult. Now it is the staff's turn to generate ideas and "help" the leader clarify the vision. While the leader is concerned with promulgating the vision, the organization is churning to develop initial staff analysis and other products. The staff presents them to the leader, who typically acknowledges the effort but issues new guidance based on how much more advanced the vision has become in the leader's mind.

In the third phase, the communication effort is in full implementation. The leader anticipates and expects action. Meanwhile, the staff is finalizing the plan for leader 'decision,' which is essentially the leader's acceptance of a particular set of actions, not a return to the initial decision whether or not to act. So for the change effort, the leader's decision to proceed with a plan and set of actions launches the change effort. Of course, the communication campaign is already in full implementation as stakeholders are engaged and have set their expectations. While the staff is measuring the *performance* of the early activities of the change effort, the leader is already measuring the *effectiveness* of the communications. For example, is the effort unified, or is there resistance from within the organization?

As the plan is set and the change effort moves to implementation, the communication effort is now at sustainment. The leader is looking ahead for what may stop the change effort in its tracks – resources, new challenges, or something else? While the organization is busy putting the plan in motion, the leader is

---

[7] This is sometimes known as "getting ahead of the boss."

now free to generate the next new idea. The organization, still in the throes of making the first change effort successful, perceives that another idea is brewing. "What now?" they ask as they re-enter the dreaded chaos phase. And so it goes…

As Figure 1 shows, one can view the communication effort as being generally one phase ahead of the change effort. In effect, the change effort is always a step behind the communication, rather than in step with it as is typically implied in both the change management and strategic communication literature. There are several implications for this. First, communication can appear poor from the member's perspective because of the churn. Staffs are accustomed to the idea that they provide the analysis and the leader makes the decision. In communication, a leader's decision always precedes the staff analysis, putting the staff in reaction mode which they do not prefer. At best, it is tolerable. At worst, it creates tremendous friction and resistance.

Second, the leader's vision development can go on indefinitely, which adds to the staff's frustration. It is not unusual for leader communications to be situation-dependent, whereas staffs want definitive, unerring guidance to help them accomplish the task of planning change. Any prevarication on the leader's part doubles the staff's time.

Third, because of the typical turnover of military leadership, it is that much easier for leaders to declare victory as they depart. In their minds, their vision is already in full implementation, minus many of the details which are assumed to work themselves out. So long as the plan is in place, everything should go smoothly. But for a similar reason, incoming leaders are just as likely to see the communication-change disparity – that what is espoused is not being enacted at the same right. The new leader may opt to pursue a new idea instead of trying to relearn all of what went into the communication effort thus far.

The above suggests that deliberate communication efforts are a different construct from change, requiring potentially different methods of development and different measures of success. The roles of leaders also appears to be different, much more hands-on in communication than in change.

Organization of this Primer

This Primer is the result of seven years of study and reflection on the case studies, combined with extensive analysis of the academic literature across a number of fields that touch on communication in organizations. These include but are not limited to organization learning, organizational culture, institution theory, organizational communication, leadership and leader development, change, organizational storytelling, management science, and many others. Each of these fields contributed important clues as to how to analyze leader and follower actions, understand how they constructed messages and why, and how to get large, complex organizations to stay aligned with them. What emerged was an understanding of what a communication effort really is, as understood in practice — a *campaign*. It is a unified effort of the organization promoting a message to achieve desired effects.

Campaigning, by its nature, takes time and effort and there is no shortcut or quick solution. Rather than a quick, shallow model or formula that makes the process look easy or approachable, a communication campaign methodology must be thoughtful and thorough. Just as it is easy for someone to poke holes in another's shaky argument, a campaign built on a quick and simplistic flowchart-style process inevitably succumbs to gaps and inconsistencies that opponents can readily exploit. As this Primer will show, in the communication arena, one's opponents have a tremendous advantage.

I organized this Primer in three major parts. The first part defines campaigns — what they are and why they are challenging -- and the leader's roles in campaigning. Chapter 1 details the challenge of communication campaigns and addresses the roles of senior leaders as organizational communicators. This is vastly different from their roles as individual communicators, dealing with how they address the public personally. Rather, it addresses their roles in setting strategic direction for the organization to communicate the leaders' messages.

Chapters 2 through 5 discuss the major elements of what is known as the *standing campaign*, the campaign for the organization's survival that begins upon inception and concludes when the organization ceases to exist (and beyond, so long as people want to bring it back). Chapter 2 covers the organization's narrative and how to derive it. What is the story of the organization? Chapter 3 addresses counter-narratives, the opposing views. How do leaders derive them and defend the organization against them? Chapter 4 covers audiences — who is the organization communicating with? Finally, Chapter 5 discusses the internal communication practices of the organization. How does it communicate, formally and informally? What factors must the leader consider when getting the organization to further the leaders' messages?

Chapter 6 through 9 present the major activities of a *named campaign* – when the leader has a particular communication purpose in mind, such as supporting a transformational change effort or helping the organization overcome a crisis or external threat. Chapter 6 discusses the personal strategy of leaders in the campaign and the leader's personal campaign strategies. Chapter 7 covers how to initial a communication campaign to intervene in the organizational environment. It encompasses development of a vision, themes, and messages for the campaign. Chapters 8 and 9 cover the campaign's launch and post-launch sustainment phases, respectively.

The nine-chapter structure corresponds to a nine seminar classes in a standard two-credit U.S. Army War College elective. When accompanied by a case study, each chapter provides enough material to cover a three-hour block of instruction. Most chapters are divided into three topics, each of which can easily provide an hour of quality dialogue. Instructors wishing to use this Primer in other settings can easily do so by selecting questions and topics that align with their particular course objectives and available time.

Chapter 1. Defining Communication Campaigns

Before getting into *what* a communication campaign is, it is important to discuss the problem that any campaigning methodology is to solve. For the US military, the problem is essentially this: *dissatisfaction with both the quality and speed of communication, resulting in an inability to achieve the desired effects.*[8] Whether it is with actors in the operational environment, among domestic audiences, or among its own membership, the military senses that it does a poor job of communicating. From ill-conceived outreach programs in Iraq and Afghanistan to the challenges of recurring crises related to sexual harassment and assault, bad news stories seem to outnumber the good.

It is easy to equate the lack of desired effects as failure. However, in dynamic and complex environments, there are many intervening factors which include the dispositions of the other actors. While there is utility in trying to improve one's own processes of communicating, as has been the goal of Department of Defense (DoD) strategic communication efforts, the problem is much bigger.

What is the Problem We Aim to Solve?

I will address the above problem statement through liberal use of the pronouns *we (us)* and *they (them)*. *We* constitutes the organization in question, although the organization's boundary may change as one learns more about the problem. For example, *we* may initially represent a single base or post, but the real problem (and therefore the real *we*) may turn out to be the U.S. Army or DoD as a whole.

Meanwhile, *they* are not the same organization, but *they* are not necessarily external, either. *They* may be: (1) a completely discrete entity composed of different individuals than *us*, (2) an overlapping entity that includes individuals both internal and

---

[8] Steve Tatham, *U.S. Governmental Information Operations and Strategic Communications: A Discredited Tool or User Failure? Implications for Future Conflict* (Carlisle, PA: Strategic Studies Institute, 2013), 64-65.

external to the organization, or (3) wholly a part of *us*, i.e., an internal subset of the organization such as a subunit or collection of members with a common identity (e.g., race, gender, interests, skills or knowledge). The composition of *they* is dynamic as any organization or collective is an open system with porous and dynamic boundaries. For example, men and women enter and leave military service every day. Therefore, *they* may be a formally named actor in the environment or may be entirely informal or *ad hoc*, such as anonymous participants in the social media community who come together in response to some event, condition, or issue.[9]

With *we* and *they* described, the following elaborate on the communication problem *we* face.

"They" aren't listening

The intended audiences are not receiving or responding to the messages sent by the organization. *They* continue life as though the message was not sent or they explicitly deny or defy the message. I offer three variants of this problem.[10]

The simplest is that that *they cannot listen*. This is a problem of means. Some audiences are remote and have limited physical access to outside media (e.g., Internet, open news sources), while others are overwhelmed with choices of media and do not monitor the channels the military is using. Thus the message is not being heard. The solution sounds similarly means-driven – add radio stations and programs, websites, news articles. Then, increase the volume by presenting our message through texts, posts, videos, and broadcasts. In theory more would hear us. But in reality, increasing communication breadth and depth takes money, time, and energy which are finite.

Compounding the above problem is the strength of opposing narratives, such that even those who receive U.S. communications are likely to reject it, or react to it in ways opposite of what was intended. In other words, *they will not listen*. What we say, they do not hear or they replace with something else. Reaching out to such

---

[9] Galvin, *Two Case Studies*, Chapter 5.
[10] Ibid., Chapters 3 and 5. This section is based on the author's experience in USAFRICOM.

audiences is intended as a gesture of goodwill, but taken as a sign of arrogance or a threat. 'We' can talk until blue in the face, the effects of such communication may be negligible.

The third is that *they are listening to others more*. In this case, *they* are neutral audiences who have equal stake in both the U.S. and opposing positions. *We* might assume such audiences are misinformed, and that *they* can be willed toward accepting the friendly message. However, the more important problem is one of *disinformation*. Perhaps *they* succumb to influence by opposing actors whose power over *them* is greater than *ours*. Or, perhaps *they* are passing on urban legends or myths that somehow seem more plausible or comforting than *our* message.

"They" are changing their actions, but not their minds

Assuming *we* reach our intended audience with our message, and it is at least willing to listen to that message, *we* do not always realize our desired effects.[11] Polling numbers or other empirical indicators, when available, may show evidence that the message is indeed out there, received and enacted upon. *They* have heard us, seen us or watched our actions, or *they* learned of it second- and third-hand from others by word-of-mouth or other media. So *they* may be changing what they do, but the evidence suggests that *they* are only doing it to placate us or deflect attention away, but not internalize the message. Therefore, *they* may likely revert to prior behaviors when *we* stop communicating or observing their behavior. Below are three possible reasons why.

The first is that *they do not wish to appear to have been influenced*. This can be for exogenous reasons—that *they* will become disgraced in the minds of others. Maintaining self-determination can be an overriding concern even among audiences who agree with *our* message. Each receiver must weigh the consequences of appearing to lose independence or become too closely associated with *our* position—damaging reputations, inviting accusations of weakness or waffling, or even encouraging opponents to target them.

---

[11] Ibid.

Audiences may also have endogenous reasons to avoid appearing to be influenced. Perhaps *they fear losing their own identity*. Agreeing with *us* on one issue calls *their* views on other issues into question. *They* might not wish to feel associated with *us* so *they* may be free to disagree on other issues. Preserving *their* autonomy means keeping some measure of distance from *us*.

Finally, *they might agree but they decline to be our messenger*. Because organizational energy is finite, it is natural for *us* to want the message to spread on its own. *We* hope, perhaps, that the message goes 'viral,' so *we* can achieve our aims more efficiently. Unfortunately, it rarely works. *They* may be reluctant to share *our* messages for us, seeing that as *our* own responsibility (or worse, *they* may inject their own viewpoints that are incorrect and expect *us* to correct the record).

"We" do not trust our own consistent delivery of the message

We want our messages to go out unchanged, unfiltered, uncorrupted, and so on. *We* know *they* will change it to suit *their* interests. But, *we* are imperfect human beings and *we* do not always repeat and share the intended message as originally crafted. Sometimes this is OK, so long as the intended meaning is conveyed. Other times, this is a problem, as the change in words can produce changes in the meaning — real or perceived by *them*. *They* may exploit those changes in ways *we* do not desire.

The all-to-common response? *We must increase control over the message*.[12] If *we* stick to the precise message, *we* will unify our communication and overwhelm *them* with *our* truth.[13] However, the modern communication environment is highly asymmetric, and *they* are not bound to the same truth.[14] Thus, increasing control over the message reduces *our* flexibility as *they* change *our* message. Worse, *our* members may interpret such controls as

---

[12] Paul Cornish, Julian Lindley-French, and Claire Yorke, *Strategic Communications and National Strategy* (London: Chatham House, Royal Institute of International Affairs, 2011), 1-2.

[13] U.S. Joint Forces Command, *Commander's Handbook for Strategic Communication and Communication Strategy*, Version 3.0 (Norfolk, VA: Joint Warfighting Center, 2010), II-13.

[14] Neville Bolt, "Strategic Communications in Crisis," *RUSI Journal*, Vol. 156, No. 4 (2011): 45 says "Carefully controlled state strategic communications are being unpicked at the seams, and states are forced increasingly into reactive postures. Speed, reach, and iconic images have becomes a toxic brew for which states have no antidote."

showing a lack of trust, inconsistent with the U.S. military's espoused philosophy of *Mission Command* that includes the creation of shared understanding, exercise of disciplined initiative, and acceptance of prudent risk.[15]

Yet, *we* cannot fully loosen the reins. In some circumstances, especially crisis situations, *we* require tighter controls because knowledge of the truth behind the message is limited to the few, and *we* must avoid inadvertently spreading rumors and misinformation. This was the case with the DoD campaign against sexual harassment and assault that was a problem for both the military's identity and its reputation with stakeholders (e.g., Congress and the public). Thus, the question for leaders is whether the internal processes of communication are aligned with the environment and leader expectations. Are levels of control over *our* messages appropriate, too strong, or too loose, therefore inhibiting the desired flow of communication or straining relationships between *our* leaders and members?

"We" do not believe our own message

If the members of the organization do not accept and believe *our* message, *they* will not share it. Worse, *they* may change it. Unfortunately, members may not tell the leader that problems exist with the message. *They* may find it easier to change it, decline to share it, or share it with little or no enthusiasm.

Why do *we* reject *our* own messages? One is when *our message means far more to our leaders than to our members.* Leaders are often advised to keep messages simple so they can be grasped easily.[16] But if the members cannot draw meaning from the messages, then they will probably reject them as *pabulum*, "insipid, simplistic, or bland."[17] Another way to express this is "PowerPoint deep," where the message is not backed up by relatable plans or strategies.[18] Perhaps the message crafted by leaders do not

---

[15] U.S. Army, *Mission Command*, Army Doctrinal Publication 6-0 (Washington, DC: U.S. Department of the Army, 2012), iv.

[16] John Baldoni, *Great Communication Secrets of Great Leaders* (New York: McGraw-Hill, 2003), 55.

[17] Merriam-Webster Online Dictionary, s.v. "Pabulum," https://www.merriam-webster.com/dictionary/pabulum (retrieved 1 August 2017).

[18] Ben Zwiebelson, "How PowerPoint Stifles Understanding, Creativity, and Innovation Within Your Organization," *Small Wars Journal*, September 4, 2012,

translate well to the front lines of the organization, or meaning was lost when making the message as broadly applicable or inclusive as possible.

Another challenge is when *our message is old or obsolete, but we keep saying it anyway*. This is a problem of reaching back too far into history. Perhaps the message was important in some past glory days or heroic rescue from a crisis. Perhaps it reflected a past period of excellence that propelled the organization to greatness at one time, or it was the bravery or heroism of *our* members with whom leaders wish current members to know about. Messages do not reinvigorate themselves, *we* must reinvigorate them to keep them fresh and relevant lest they become stale and lose meaning.

And then there are times when *our messages are undeniably wrong*. In other words, *we* seem to be kidding *ourselves* and *we* know it. Sometimes, *we* do this to hide from the truth – *we* do not want to admit failure even though we should. More often, however, *we* do this to inspire *ourselves* and blunt the criticisms and negativity coming from *them*. *We* are buying time and space to correct problems and regroup, much like a losing team taking a timeout to shift the momentum of a game. The message may be wrong in a literal sense, but the intended meaning is more important. The question is how to convince *ourselves* to get past the literal.

WHAT IS A COMMUNICATION CAMPAIGN?

When one thinks of planning and implementing military campaigns, a number of planning constructs often come to mind. What are the major operations that comprise the campaign? How will the mission be divided among the forces allocated? How will activities be synchronized horizontally and vertically over time? How will the force commander measure success? What is the definition of victory? Campaigns are assumed to be complex and often take extended amounts of time, therefore developing campaign plans is a significant undertaking. Planners, however, have access to a significant body of knowledge – theory, doctrine, and practical experience – to build campaign plans that maximize

---

http://smallwarsjournal.com/jrnl/art/how-powerpoint-stifles-understanding-creativity-and-innovation-within-your-organization?page=1 (retrived 3 August 2017).

the chance of meeting the mission and reducing risk. The US military often applies the campaign metaphor to other strategic-level activities as well, including major organizational change efforts, response to significant external and internal crises, and major joint/interagency activities. Division of labors and coordination mechanisms, where possible to define, help guide the total effort toward a campaign objective.

The campaign metaphor can also be applied to organized communication efforts whose purpose is for the organization to speak and act in unison. The goals may be less tangible than for traditional campaigns – e.g., *we* need to change *their* hearts and minds -- but the need for strategy, planning, and adaptability is the same. Marketing campaigns aim to capture people's attention and influence their purchasing behaviors rather than capturing geographic territory. Recruiting campaigns encourage eligible people to join the organization as members. Campaigns against sexual harassment or to prevent military suicide root out problems from within by sharing information, reinforcing organizational values, and assembling a unified effort to fix what is wrong. These campaigns are every bit as complex and require similar understandings of organizing and synchronizing the effort, clarifying goals, measuring success, and declaring victory.

Communications campaigns promote the organization and guide how organizations as whole promote, defend, and adapt their narratives for a specified purpose, while targeting other organizations and their narratives. The campaign symbolizes the whole organization fighting to accomplish a strategic mission, but composed of hundreds or thousands of interdependent but often conflicting or chaotic activities. The metaphor allows leaders to think strategically about the desired effects on the environment, rather than overemphasizing measures of performance. It recognizes that the whole organization communicates, thus the campaigns provide vision and strategic direction that the entire organization can use without unduly constraining or limited communication. Finally, the campaign is a multi-level construct that permits nesting of subordinate campaigns, relying on trust vertically, horizontally, and among individual members.

However, there is an important caveat to the campaign metaphor. In typical military usage, campaigns are thought of as strategically broad in scope and all-encompassing. When there is a theater campaign, everyone in the theater operates on that one campaign, and all subordinate elements' activities are tightly nested. Communications campaigns are different in that they are not necessarily all-encompassing at a theater level. Each organization, at echelon, conducts its own campaigns — be in the national level (e.g., President and Congress), Department of Defense, joint community, services, commands, all the way down to the unit level. Each organization is unique and communicates that uniqueness to serve organizational purposes. Recruiting is an example — all military organizations recruit but each unit at echelon develops strategies and communications to recruit for the unit.

Yet, campaigns among military organizations are interdependent. *Nesting* of campaigns stresses the importance of lower-level organizations inheriting and subsuming communications from above into their own. It helps large organizations speak and act as one. Lower-level campaigns are also interdependent in the horizontal sense — units will often copy or mimic what other like units are saying and doing. The implication is that *an organization's campaigns are all-encompassing for the organization*. The organization is its own theater — of which higher-level organizations serve as important actors (or rather, stakeholders as Chapter 4 will show).

WHAT ARE DIFFERENT TYPES OF COMMUNICATION CAMPAIGNS?

But not all campaigns in an organization are alike. There are those that the leader designates and then there's all the other 'stuff' that organizations say and do without the leader's direct involvement. The fact is, organizations are *always* communicating regardless of the presence of on-going deliberate communication efforts. Organizations have enduring opposing messages facing them, their audiences change little or evolve slowly, and many of its processes and systems for communicating are already embedded. In effect, the organization is constantly campaigning – to garner resources, promote itself, or fight for survival.

This is the organization's *standing campaign*. See Figure 2. Standing campaigns explain the organizational context as the sum of the answers to four essential questions: (1) what is our message, (2) what are the opposing messages, (3) who are we communicating with, and (4) how do we communicate? An organization only has one standing campaign whose purpose is the organization's survival. It began when the organization formed and will end only when the organization ceases to exist.

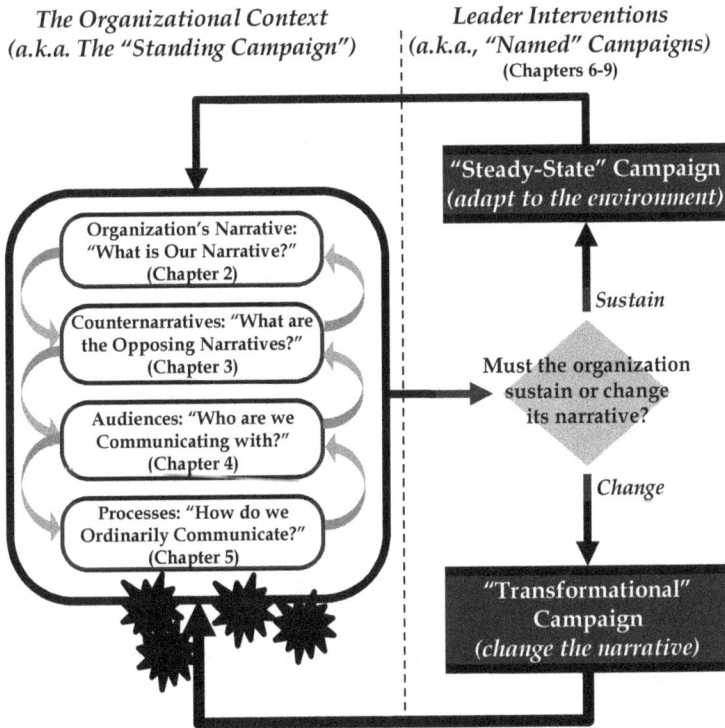

Figure 2. Standing and Named Campaigns[19]

The standing campaign draws from the enacted culture and climate of the organization. It captures the enduring identity of the organization and its embedded habits and practices, which may differ from any particular leader's wishes. For example, the leader may prefer that the organization become 'innovative' and 'cutting-edge,' but the standing campaign may reflect a deep-rooted culture where organizational members are more

---

[19] Original graphic by author.

accustomed to 'continuity,' 'stability,' or 'reliability.' Even when members agree that becoming innovative is vital for the organization's survival, as a collective the organization's membership will follow what is familiar or comfortable and abide by the culture. The inverse is also true – an organization may have been founded as cutting-edge and entrepreneurial but a new leader may desire a more consistent and predictable culture to maintain the organization's competitive advantage. The members will likely resist because the leader's perspective differs from what the organization has valued.

The standing campaign is hardly static. In fact, it is dynamic. It captures everything (and I mean *everything*) the organization — its leaders *and* members--says and does. As the organization evolves over time, so too does its identity, behaviors, processes, and so on. Thus, the standing campaign captures the history of the organization, which I call the *organizational narrative* (more on 'narrative' in Chapter 2). The narrative constantly builds through both the words and actions of members and how members remember (or misremember) and share them. The process of building the narrative occurs absent, even despite, leader intervention.

But leaders do intervene. They are expected to if the organization is not performing to stakeholder or customer desires, or is otherwise unsatisfactory in the leader's eyes. Intervening is an act of communication, representing a type of campaign intended to change the direction of the organization and ensure its continued survival. I called these *named campaigns* because they commonly have a name or moniker to identify them. Named campaigns are means by which the leader: (a) keeps the organization aligned with the environment, or (b) changes it course. These result in two types of named campaigns, each shown in Figure 2. and each representing a different purpose and desired outcome.

Keeping the organization aligned is the function of what I call a *steady-state campaign*. Such campaigns allow leaders to cause the organization to remain aligned with the environment and sustain its competitive advantage. The organization changes, but the change is more incremental and evolutionary with the intent of better posturing the existing organization for success. Steady-state campaigns may serve any of the following purposes: correcting problems or bad organizational habits, addressing crises, confronting new threats or adversaries, changing or renewing or restating organizational messages, and promoting new or improved products and services.

In contrast, leaders use *transformational campaigns* to deliberately change the identity of the organization. These campaigns inform members and organizational stakeholders of the purposes for change and the ways and means of accomplishing it. Transformational campaigns provide vision and strategic direction to garner support and acceptance while overcoming barriers to change emanating from the organization's standing campaign and outside resistance. These campaigns are much more complex and difficult than steady-state campaigns because the standing campaign is highly resilient.

I now add two more essential questions to communication campaigning: (5) what are the leader's roles in named campaigns, and (6) how do leaders initiate and implement them? Leaders cannot merely declare a named campaign's existence and assume any good will come of it. Having a poorly named campaign is worse than having no named campaign, because the poor campaign's existence will be embedded in the standing campaign. It will become a story that members will share as a warning to other members that change is bad, leaders are incompetent, or the organization is not worth one's commitment and energy. Leaders must therefore show appreciation of the standing campaign and plan their named campaigns appropriately.

What does right look like? One can look to the example of U.S. Africa Command (USAFRICOM). The announcement of its creation in February 2007 was resoundingly jeered, and the fledgling organization faced intense scrutiny and criticism throughout its early days. Yet within two years, USAFRICOM succeeded in changing the minds of many U.S. and African stakeholders and overcame much of the negative, reactionary opinions the announcement generated through a concerted communication campaign.[20] The campaign, which the author

---

[20] William E. Ward, "Strategic Communication at Work," *Leader to Leader* 59 (December 2011): 33-38.

helped develop and implement, succeeded because of a thorough understanding of the communication environment, a well-crafted message, and synchronized delivery by the entire organization, not just the commander, over the course of three years. The result was two-fold: (1) broad acceptance of USAFRICOM among key U.S. and African stakeholders that facilitated the command's mission, and (2) the quieting of other critics.

Therefore, creating communication campaigns, which are therefore *named* campaigns, first requires understanding the organization's one and only *standing* campaign. Embedded within it is everything that the organization is, has said, and has done that the leader finds dissatisfying.

When properly analyzed, the standing campaign provides leaders with a wealth of information about the organization — how it sees itself, what are its strengths and vulnerabilities, and what is its identity and history. If leaders wish to align organizations with their visions, then they enact named campaigns to do so, using well-planned and well-enacted themes and messages that explain to internal and external audiences what the leader wants and why.

WHAT ARE THE LEADER'S COMMUNICATION ROLES?

Leaders play prominent roles in the development and sustainment of all the organization's communication, but how leaders enact those roles depends greatly on the leaders. Some leaders prefer to be more public while others prefer to remain in the background and allow members to speak and act more on the organization's behalf. Still others are flexible, and change their communication profile based on the circumstances. Regardless of how the leaders personally communicate, however, there are four common duties that all leaders perform with respect to an organization's communication. Leaders may delegate specific responsibilities, but leaders cannot delegate the legitimacy that enables members to communicate on behalf of the organization. When the leader allows a subordinate (e.g., spokesperson) to speak on behalf of the organization, the leader legitimizes that communication. When the spokesperson makes a mistake, the communication still reflects upon the leader who must decide whether to personally issue a correction, direct the spokesperson to correct the mistake, or underwrite the error and move on.

The following four roles stem from the legitimacy conferred upon the organization's leader (or leadership team in cases where formal leadership roles are divided). The first role is *embodiment of the organization*.[21] Senior leaders adopt a working identity that is congruent with the organization's identity. In essence, whatever the organization sees as salient, the leader personally adopts. Leaders of professional organizations, for example, must be consummate professionals and conduct themselves accordingly. Similarly, one expects leaders of service organizations to embody the organization's service mission and avoid appearing to act in self-serving ways.

Second is that the leader is *steward of the organization's narrative*.[22] While leaders may not be able to control or manage all the organization's communication, they are its caretakers by virtue of the legitimacy they confer upon members. Therefore, they have the personal responsibilities to assess the quality of the standing campaign and determine the need for named campaigns.

Once a leader decides upon a named campaign, the leader must own it. Leaders are the *champions of the organization's campaigns*. Even when the need for a named campaign is initiated and exercised by members, it is the leader who champions it through an organizational climate that permits the campaign's implementation and prevents the erection of barriers against it. Or, the leader may elect to assert ownership of the campaign and in turn confer direct legitimacy to the members conducting it. Although delivery of messages may be delegated, audiences presume leader endorsement. Any misstatements or mishaps the organization says or does reflects back to the senior leadership.[23]

Finally, leaders serve as *governors of the organization's communication process*. Leaders own the internal processes of

---

[21] This duty is a combination of the *figurehead* and *spokesperson* roles described in Henry Mintzberg, *The Nature of Managerial Work* (Englewood Cliffs, NJ: Prentice-Hall, 1973).

[22] This duty is derived from the work of Don M. Snider in relation to stewardship of the profession. See Snider, "The U.S. Army as a Profession."

[23] John Kotter, *Leading Change* (Boston, MA: Harvard University Press, 1996).

communication, regardless of how much they actually exercise control over it. They must account for how organizations ordinarily engage with their environments – formally and informally. If the communication process is not working, the leader must fix it or assume the risks of communication failure.[24]

---

[24] This combines Mintzberg's decisional and interpersonal roles in driving the organization's culture and internal processes. However, in military organizations this duty is often delegated to a deputy or chief of staff.

CHAPTER 2. WHAT IS OUR NARRATIVE?

We human beings are storytellers by nature. So it is not surprising that because organizations are composed of humans, organizations have many, many stories to tell. When shared among members and non-members alike, these stories help reinforce desired behaviors, sustain member and stakeholder expectations, or uplift and inspire. They also do the inverse, such as warning members about what is undesired.[25] The result is that members learn what it means to be a member.

But what about the organization itself? Does it have a story? The answer is clearly yes, as people routinely take words and actions by members and characterize the organization as the actor. What the U.S. Army says and does differs from what any individual member (even the Army's Chief of Staff) says or does. We celebrate the organization's birthdays and anniversaries, great moments, crises and recoveries, and other milestones; or we pillory the organization for its bureaucracy or various missteps and scandals. And so, like a person, an organization has a history.

But, is there only one story of the organization or is it many? I argue there is only one, and I will use the history of an American football team to demonstrate.

THE STORY OF THE PITTSBURGH STEELERS

Formed in 1933 as the Pirates, they renamed themselves as the Steelers six years later in honor of Pittsburgh's long ties with the steel industry.[26] On the field, they struggled for several decades, posting only occasional winning records and making the playoffs only twice through 1971. But their fortunes improve suddenly in the 1970s after a famous play (the so-called Immaculate Reception) that propelled the team to its first playoff victory ever. By 1975, the Steelers were a powerhouse team that would win

---

[25] Joanne Martin, Martha S. Feldman, Mary Jo Hatch, and Sim B. Sitkin, "The Uniqueness Paradox of Organizational Stories," *Administrative Science Quarterly* 28 (1983): 428-453.

[26] Pittsburgh Steelers' history is compiled from Encyclopaedia Brittanica, s.v. "Pittsburgh Steelers." Available at: https://www.britannica.com/topic/Pittsburgh-Steelers [Accessed 20 September 2017] and ProFootballReference.com, s.v. 'Pittsburgh Steelers.' Available at: https://www.pro-football-reference.com/teams/pit/ [Accessed 20 September 2017].

four Super Bowls in six years. They would remain generally competitive over the subsequent decades, before winning their fifth and sixth Super Bowls in the 2000s.

Off the field, the Steelers are one of the most followed and popular sports franchises in the US. The Steelers brand ranks very high for merchandise sales, distribution of fan base across the country, and franchise net worth.[27] One of the more recognized symbols of any US sports team is the Steelers' 'Terrible Towel,' a yellow hand towel with the team's logo waved at Steeler games.[28] Steeler fans have also displayed these towels as a symbol of the city while on vacation, on military deployments, or when hosting major world or media events.[29]

If one were to ask a casual Steelers' fan to tell the team's story, it would likely begin with the Immaculate Reception and Super Bowl years, ignoring the previous uninteresting history. But of course, that history counted for something. For example, had the Steelers not suffered through several last-place seasons in the 1960s, they would not have been able to draft some of the players who would lead them through the glory days of the 1970s. Older or more knowledgeable Steelers' fans might reach back through the lean years. Younger fans? Their first-person experiences might be limited to their last two Super Bowls victories in this century.

This example illustrates that there is only one story, but that different people find parts of it more salient than others. They therefore construct what sound like different stories they reflect their personal connections with the organization.[30] What will

---

[27] Badenhausen, Kurt. 'Full List: The World's 50 Most Valuable Sports Team 2017,' *Forbes.com*, 12 July 2017. Available at:
https://www.forbes.com/sites/kurtbadenhausen/2017/07/12/full-list-the-worlds-50-most-valuable-sports-teams-2017/#fffa3514a05c [Accessed 20 September 2017] and Michael Lewis, 'NFL Fan Base and Brand Rankings 2017,' *Sports Analytics Research from Mike Lewis*, 17 June 2017. Available at: https://scholarblogs.emory.edu/esma/2017/06/17/nfl-fan-base-and-brand-rankings-2017/ [Accessed 20 September 2017]
[28] 'History of the Terrible Towel,' *VisitPittsburgh.com*. Available at:
https://www.visitpittsburgh.com/things-to-do/spectator-sports/terrible-towel/ [Accessed 20 September 2017]
[29] For example, see Daveynin, 'Terrible Towel around the World,' *Flickr.com* [photo gallery]. Available at:
https://www.flickr.com/photos/daveynin/galleries/72157622407316807/ [Accessed 6 October 2017].
[30] Mary Jo Hatch, "The Dynamics of Organizational Culture, *Academy of Management Review* 18, no. 4 (October 1993): 657-693.

become clear in later chapters is how leaders, as individual members of the organization, project their personal perspectives on the organization's story—determining what elements they consider salient, and crafting their version of the story from them.

An organization's standing campaign is therefore rooted in its one unique story. It tell the story of the organization from its beginning to the present, and the story continues to grow until the organization ceases to exist—and may continue on through the memories (real and imagined), whether of former members or others who only heard of the organization having existed. The story captures the organization's evolving purposes from why it was formed to why it remains in existence at present. How has its mission, organization, and resources changed? What it has done well or poorly? What crises or changes it faced and how it responded? How does the organization as a whole interact with its subcomponents or members? What lessons did it learn? What mistakes does it habitually repeat? Often, the interesting, distressing, and the unusual are better remembered than the day-to-day routine activities. When members share the organization's story among themselves, they summarize it by drawing on the more exciting parts, emphasizing the conflict, tension, tough decisions, and resolutions; while some of the rest are set aside and possible forgotten over time.

The result is that part of the story worth remembering and passing on, even if the story is no longer complete. This version of the organization's story is what I call the *narrative*.

WHAT IS *NARRATIVE* AND WHY IS IT IMPORTANT?

A *narrative* is "a representation of a particular situation or process in such a way as to reflect or conform to an overarching set of aims or values."[31] Narrative is an *artifact*[32] of the organizational culture, stemming from the underlying assumptions to provide the rationale *why* the organization says and does things certain ways. When members speak or act in alignment with the narrative, the communication is more natural

---

[31] Oxford Online Dictionary, s.v. "Narrative."
[32] As defined by Edgar H. Schein, *Organizational Culture and Leadership,* 4th Edition (San Francisco: Jossey-Bass, 2010), 17-19.

and the members will be more effective at communicating. When they do not align, members may get uncomfortable delivering the message, and the receivers will notice.

The challenge for leaders is capturing as much of the narrative as possible. It is difficult to do, because organizations rarely have its full narrative documented and neatly available in a repository, and members will be inconsistent when telling their versions of it. In military organizations, leaders often have little first-hand experience with the organizations they lead, and have limited available time to reconstruct the narrative by themselves. Fortunately, the narrative is composed of the most salient parts of the organization's story and there are ways of identifying what members and external stakeholders consider to be salient. By capturing these elements, leaders can build an approximation of the narrative sufficiently useful to assess and adjust the standing campaign.

The narrative has two components, as Figure 3 shows. The first is the *organizational identity*, which is how members answer the question, *who are we?*[33] The second is the *organizational image*, how the organization projects itself to the environment. These components present a number of claims that members of the organization make, claims of who the organization is, and why the organization is superior (or inferior) to other organizations.[34]

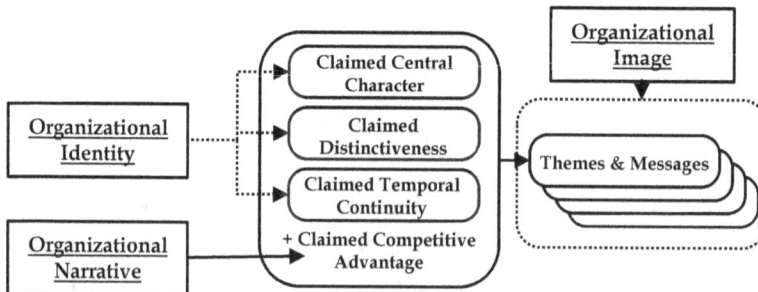

Figure 3. Components of an Organization's Narrative[35]

---

[33] Stuart Albert and David A. Whetten, "Organizational Identity," *Research in Organizational Behavior* 7 (1985): 263-295.

[34] The relationship of identity and image stems from Hatch & Schultz, Figure 2 (p. 995).

[35] Original graphic by author.

How do we Identify Ourselves as an 'Organization'?

An *organizational identity* establishes a baseline of behavior and belief, analogous to individual identity. For example, a Soldier asserts, "I am a Soldier." By virtue of that statement, the Soldier establishes an individual identity. In a similar way, when a military organization declares, "we are a profession," it establishes a collective identity as a profession, one that encompasses all its members.

However, asserting an organizational identity is does not mean that members will automatically accept it. Just because the U.S. Army says it is a profession does not necessarily make it so.[36] Also, just because the U.S. Army says it is a profession does not necessarily mean all members automatically see themselves as professionals.[37] Therefore, the literature addresses organizational identities as *claimed*, rather than definitely determined the same way as for individual identities. For the U.S. Army, there are many claims made, such as being: (1) a professional organization, (2) a Landpower force, (3) an all-Volunteer force, (4) a cutting-edge technologically-savvy force, (5) a victor of many wars and therefore a force to be reckoned with, (6) a force for good around the world, (7) a caring, respectful, and inclusive organization, (8) an opportunity to grow and gain important life skills, and so on. Each of these are *identity claims*, characteristics that members believe and assert are part of the organization's story.[38] Albert and Whetten (1985) established three types of organizational identity claims:[39]

- *Claimed central character.* This constitutes an organization's avowed essence. The U.S. Army, for example, describes its

---

[36] Don M. Snider, *Once Again, the Challenge to the U.S. Army During a Defense Reduction: To Remain a Military Profession*, Professional Military Ethics Monograph Series, Volume 4 (Carlisle, PA: Strategic Studies Institute, 2012), 5.

[37] Ibid., also Don M. Snider, "The U.S. Army as a Profession," in *The Future of the Army Profession*, 2nd ed., Don M. Snider and ed. Lloyd Matthews (New York: McGraw-Hill, 2005), 1-17.

[38] David Whetten, "Albert and Whetten Revisited: Strengthening the Concept of Organizational Identity," *Journal of Management Inquiry* 15, no. 3 (September 2006), 220.

[39] Albert and Whetten, "Organizational Identity," 265.

central character as a "profession of arms"[40] and has incorporated it into published doctrine, statements of leaders, human resource management systems and process, and professional military education.

- *Claimed distinctiveness.* This separates one organization from others like it. Each of the services can claim to be within the profession of arms, but the U.S. Army separates itself through its unique "contribution[s] to America's [L]andpower,"[41] while the other services do likewise for their chosen domains (e.g., air, sea, space, and recently cyber).

- *Claimed temporal continuity (i.e., its connection with history).* The organization's identity should remain persistent, meaning little changed over time. It should not undergo continuous transformation, although some evolution is appropriate and expected. The U.S. Army draws heavily on its long history of heroism and victory to celebrate excellence, sustain morale, and attract new members.

In military organizations, central character claims are very important. Organizations may celebrate their histories or distinguish themselves by association with a branch, functional area, series, or community of practice; but most identify themselves by their mission above all else. It is the mission that orients the organization's activities; determines ideal leaders and members; sets expectations for skills, knowledge, and behaviors; and set the organization's boundary with the environment. Thus, organizational self-awareness is important, otherwise members are likely to feed leaders with only favorable stories and bias the narrative. Identity claims include both the bad and the good. What undesirable aspects of the organization are so imbued as to be part of the culture? Are there ways that the organization is distinctively dysfunctional? Is hiding bad news, withholding information from the leadership, or failing to promulgate leader

---

[40] Raymond T. Odierno, "Foreword: The Profession of Arms," *Military Review* 90, Special Edition on the Profession of Arms (September 2011): 2–4; and Department of the Army, *The Army*, Army Doctrinal Publication 1 (Washington, DC: Department of the Army, November 2012) (hereafter, *ADP 1*).
[41] *ADP 1*.

communications internally part of the organization's central character? Are there significant negative historical events whose impact on the organization has endured, such as mission failures, scandals, embarrassments, or other problems? What about bad habits (e.g., broken processes or routine poor decisions)?

HOW DO ORGANIZATIONS PRESENT THEMSELVES TO THE ENVIRONMENT?

The second component of narrative is how the organization projects these identity claims internally and externally to establish and sustain a desirable image and reputation. How others perceive the organization is very important to leaders, especially if the perceptions differ from the organization's identity or what the leaders would like. The concept of *organizational image* has a long history in the literature, but Gioia, Schulz, and Corley (2000) presented six different types based on, shown in Figure 4.

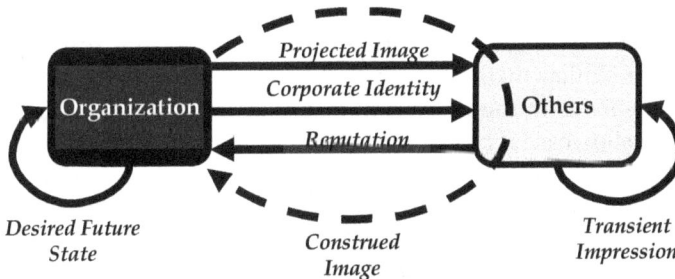

Figure 4. Six Types of Organizational Image[42]

The *projected image*[43] is the image that organizations (especially their leaders) promulgate to others. It may or may not match the real state of the organization, nor does it necessarily align with the organization's identity. It may be more aspirational

---

[42] Original graphic by author based on Gioia, Dennis A., Majken Schultz, and Kevin G. Corley, "Organizational identity, image, and adaptive instability." *Academy of Management Review* 25, no. 1 (2000): 63-81.

[43] More recent literature has merged Gioia, Schulz, & Corley's *projected image* with *corporate identity*, such as John M. Balmer, Kyoko Fukukawa, and Edmund R. Gray, "The Nature and Management of Ethical Corporate Identity: A Commentary on Corporate Identity, Corporate Social Responsibility, and Ethics," *Journal of Business Ethics*, Vol. 76, No. 1 (November 2007): 7-15. Also, Gioia, Schulz, and Corley treated *corporate identity* and *desired future image* as varieties of projected image. This treatment views the six types as distinct but related, as they reflect different uses by leaders.

than realistic.[44] Many communications from U.S. military leaders to the public or Congress seek to project an image, normally favorable, of the military, whether to promote particular programs or operations, or to enhance the standing of the military in public opinion. When the situation is negative, military leaders will normally attempt to project an image that the situation is under control or that the military is taking corrective action.

Corporate identity is akin to marketing. The corporate identity is a purposeful presentation of the organization through symbols such as logos, slogans, and other means to convince others to view the organization consistently with the organization's own self-identity. Corporate identity differs from projected images based on context. The projected image is based on context, such as events, situations, and who specifically are the Others in the Figure, whereas the corporate identity avoids context.[45] For example, the U.S. Army may employ a projected image of service and patriotism through visuals of Soldiers on duty in contemporary operations, through connections with history, or via other similar methods designed to show others what the U.S. Army is about in the present time. Conversely, the U.S. Army's slogans showcase its corporate identity. Enduring mantras such as "Be All You Can Be" (1980-2001) and "Army Strong" (2006-2015), while not conveying a perceptual image of the organization by themselves, attracted attention and conveyed the Army's claimed organizational identity in just a few words.

Reputation is defined as the "collective judgments by outsiders of an organization's actions and achievements,"[46] which constitutes the actual perceptions held by the Others. There are three components to a reputation: (a) *being well known*, such that the Others have visibility of the organization and a common perception of what it is; (b) *being known for something*, capturing the extent to which the Others judge the organization as satisfying a need; and (c) *generalized favorability* which is the degree to which

---

[44] Gioia, Schulz, and Corley, 67.

[45] Ibid.

[46] Ibid., 65; also Jane E. Dutton and Janet M. Dukerich, "Keeping an Eye on the Mirror: Image and Identity in Organizational Adaptation," *The Academy of Management Journal* 34, no. 3 (September 1991), 547-548.

Others generate positive feelings for the organization.[47] All three can be positive or negative, but it is not necessarily the case that organizations desire all three. Sometimes it is better to be well known and disliked than not be known.

The *construed image* is the image organizational members perceive or assume that others have of the organization. This image may or may not match the actual perceptions held.[48] In many ways, this serves as a proxy for full knowledge of one's reputation because an organization cannot always know with certainty how Others perceive it. For example, impressions of the U.S. military among foreign populations may be important to set conditions for future operations, but there may be little opportunity to engage those populations directly. The construed image might therefore appear as a best guess derived from polling data or other indirect sources. However, organizations must avoid biases, preconceived notions, or misperceptions. For example, after 9/11 the U.S. government discovered that its construed image as a benevolent world leader was severely misaligned with its actual reputation among the Muslim world.[49] Leaders should therefore exercise caution that the construed image is less reliable than a solid assessment of reputation. Using a construed image as a basis for narrative analysis therefore constitutes an assumption to be validated.

Reputation is difficult to change. The fifth form of image, *transient impression* demonstrates this, as it constitutes impressions acquired by Others proximate to the organization's words and actions. It differs from reputation in that transient impressions emerge from individual events; these impressions can prove irrelevant to a person's perception of the organization.[50] On the other hand, the accumulation of transient impressions can, over time, succeed in changing the organization's reputation.

The final form of image is the *desired future state*. This is essentially the image that the organization wishes to project,

---

[47] Lange, Lee, and Dai, "Organizational Reputation," 155.
[48] Dutton and Dukerich, "Keeping an Eye," 547.
[49] For example, Fareed Zakaria, "The Politics of Rage: Why do They Hate Us?" *Newsweek.com*, October 14, 2001, http://www.newsweek.com/politics-rage-why-do-they-hate-us-154345 (accessed 10 September 2015).
[50] Ibid.

orienting Others to how the organization wants to be seen.[51] For present purposes, this will become very important when discussing the named campaign in later chapters.

HOW DO ORGANIZATIONS CLAIM TO BE BETTER THAN OTHER ORGANIZATIONS?

Thus far, this chapter has focused on what constitutes the basis for an organization's narrative, or the nouns and verbs of its communication. The organization *is* this, *does* that, and *says* something about itself, ostensibly to promote itself to Others. In a competitive environment, however, it is not enough to say that one is good or great, but that one is better than another in some fashion. In essence, leaders also need a vocabulary of adjectives and adverbs that helps leaders say *we are number one!*

A good framework that is relevant for military organizations comes from a 1994 review of military readiness for the post-Cold War environment in which John Collins of the Congressional Research Service derived a set of principles of preparedness that allow military organizations to state their *competitive advantage,* which is how the military sees itself as superior or uniquely postured compared to others.[52] This is analogous to how competitive advantage is defined in the private sector as the capability to provide better products or services at lower costs to the consumer.[53] For military purposes, however, the advantage is not ordinarily exercised in a measured way, rather it is a measure of assumed potential to perform the mission when required.

The below lists eight principles of preparedness that permit comparison between military organizations. These were adapted from Collins' original work and are used at the U.S. Army War College as a way of expressing capabilities, requirements, and risk.[54] Their relative importance depends on the military

---

[51] Gioia, Schulz, and Corley, 67.

[52] Collins.

[53] Robert M. Grant, "The Resource-Based Theory of Competitive Advantage: Implications for Strategy Formulation," *California Management Review* 33, no. 3 (Spring 1991): 114-135.

[54] Thomas P. Galvin, *Military Preparedness*, 3rd Ed., Faculty Paper (Carlisle, PA: Department of Command, Leadership, and Management, November 2018).

organization and its context, however taking risk in any one presents a strategic vulnerability.[55] The principles follow:

- *Alignment with Roles and Missions* – How well organized, equipped, and trained is the organization to fulfill its assigned responsibilities? Readiness is perishable and environment is dynamic, alignment goes beyond the specified capabilities defined in the organizational structure, but also its regional expertise, interoperability, and versatility.

- *Sufficient* – Does the organization have sufficient manpower and materiel to fulfill assigned roles, functions, and missions in designated regions? The raw numbers of ready units are only part of the answer, which includes how many of them can deploy where needed to influence the situation and seize initiative.

- *Regionally Expert* – To what extent is the organization organized, equipped, and trained to accomplish missions in particular geographic regions? Today, steady-state shaping and cultural awareness are recognized as vital enabling activities, ideally to preclude future conflict. Regional expertise is highly perishable.

- *Overmatching* – Are manpower, weapons, equipment, and supplies superior to those of prospective opponents? Modernization brings new materiel capabilities to sustain such overmatch, but there is also a human dimension. Leader development, education, resiliency and fitness also contribute.

- *Interoperable* – Does the force mix must maximize the strengths and minimize the weaknesses of its parts? Most interoperability efforts focus on one dimension at a time – active-reserve or interservice or coalitions, etc. As a

---

[55] Thomas P. Galvin, "A First Principles Approach to Readiness," *ARMY* 67, no. 8 (August 2016): 16-18.

principle, interoperability is about pursuing plug-and-play capabilities versatile enough to adapt to any situation.

- *Mobilizable and Sustainable* – Does the organization's real property and outsourced capabilities facilitate essential training and furnish critical support for operations? Along with daily installation support and peacetime support capabilities, this principle also addresses surge capabilities necessary to set the theater and project national power. A strong and flexible industrial base provides additional generating capacity toward urgent operational needs. Host nation access and support are vital for establishing and sustaining lines of communication.

- *With Foresight* – How well does (or can) the organization balance short-term with long-term requirements, such as ensuring proper manning and equipping for today while continuously modernizing for the future? This principle speaks directly to risks associated with trading current unit readiness for modernization. Balance is critical.

- *With Will to be Ready* – Is the organization (and the nation and defense enterprise over it) postured for readiness, i.e., can acquire, operate, maintain, and otherwise support being ready? Will is more than financial sufficiency. It includes all peacetime diplomatic, economic, and institutional enablers from international agreements to strong civil-military relations that communicate how the nation is committed to uphold its strategic interests, and will employ military means if necessary. All these tangibles and intangibles represent the will in times of peace to be ready.

It is important to include both claims of advantage and *disadvantage*, or how the organization is inferior to others. Claims of inferiority often represent the difference between the organization's desired image and its actual reputation, and can also exemplify the gaps and inconsistencies within the organization's standing campaign.

Leaders must also consider other basis of comparison beyond the symmetric view of one organization vs. another like one. There are also comparisons between an organization's present state and a past one, such as how the provision or denial of adequate resources causes the organization to be less prepared than before, and therefore constitutes a competitive disadvantage.

ASSEMBLING THE NARRATIVE

The collection of identity claims, image, and competitive advantage claims provide a foundation for constructing a narrative for the organization. This narrative should not be considered complete, rather it constitutes an approximation of the organization's standing narrative. This is because the true narrative includes everything about the organization, important and unimportant. The approximation should be about the important factors, those that are essential for leaders to communicate or change.

However, it is not sufficient to list all the claims and call it a narrative. Lists do not provide meaning. A narrative is a story and should be assembled as such. The narrative is a passage of prose that tells a story about the organization as it is, and not necessarily what leaders or members want it to be. That will be reserved for the named campaigns which will be leader interventions into the organization and will challenge those aspects of the standing narrative that leaders wish to address.

An important point is that leaders do not have to release or publicize the narrative. It may contain controversial points about the organization that can be damaging to the reputation if made public. For example, the narrative may acknowledge flaws in the organization or contradict the leaders' public statements. On the other hand, leaders may not wish to be restrictive or limit transparency if the content presents a useful critique or identifies problems that are externally known. Therefore, the decision on what to release and what to entrust to specific members of the organization is an important and complex one. This will become apparent in later chapters discussing the initiation and implementation of named campaigns.

Combining identity and competitive advantage claims into a narrative is like saying, *this is who 'we' are and why 'you' should listen and believe us*. For example, a military force may want to deter an adversary. The force could claim a history of victory over similar adversaries in past and that its central character is one of being prepared (e.g., capable, postured, and willing) to fight again. Assembled into a narrative, the organization can develop messages – words and actions – that convince the adversary to back down. These messages are made convincing precisely because they originate from the narrative that captures what the organization believes in most about itself.

Unfortunately, this is not a one-sided affair. *We* do not have total control over the environment. Adversaries have their own narratives, too, and one can assume they will not simply back down because of our claims of preparedness. Rather, they will attempt to discredit our narrative and make our identity claims appear false or irrelevant. Thus, the next step in deriving the standing campaign is to assess what others are saying about our organization that differs from our claims, and why.

Chapter 3. What are the Opposing Narratives (Counternarratives)?

Everything an organization <u>says</u>, <u>does</u>, or <u>is</u> can and will be used against it.

Everything an organization <u>does not say</u>, <u>does not do</u>, or <u>is not</u> also can and will be used against it.

These two sentences may sound deeply cynical, but they reflect an unfortunate truth. The communication environment is fueled by negativity. Controversy draws attention and scandal sells. Anger and emotion often outperform civil dialogue.

It is simple to explain. It takes individuals a lifetime to build and sustain their persona and establish their credibility. They reconstruct and change their identities over time, and when they do they must work diligently to remain consistent in their words and actions. Attacking such a person requires nothing more than identifying a single 'flaw', removing it from context, and crafting a message that calls the individual's persona and credibility into question. The 'flaw' can be real, merely perceived, or completely fabricated; it matters little so long as the message succeeds in casting doubt in the minds of others regarding the character and intentions of the target.

Grossly unfair? Yes. Aggravating for the target? You bet. Is this new because of social media and the like? Absolutely not. This game is as old as human history, reflecting how people have always sought to separate *us* from *them*—other tribes, nations, political parties, or other collective who *we* perceived as threatening—using stories. Mass media and today's social media has merely made it easier for more individuals to join in the global information sphere and attack others from a distance (and often anonymously).

Organizations have it tough, because organizations operate in a complex competitive environment that causes them and their members to occasionally speak or act in inconsistent or erroneous ways. They want to speak and act with one voice, but in practice this is hard. Meanwhile, competition means that all organizations, societies, etc. have opponents whose interests are more efficiently served by pointing out others' flaws than promoting themselves and their narratives. The bad news spreads as mass audiences find them interesting and plausible compared to good news stories. The resulting volume of negative communication directed at organizations can be immense, particularly in times of crisis when the organization faces greater scrutiny.

The temptation that leaders must avoid is going after each individual critic or message. That is like playing a losing game of *whack-a-mole*, with the organization expending all its energy countering negative messages coming at them from many directions. It is frustrating for leaders and overall very ineffective at countering the adversarial views.

A better approach is to trace these messages back to their originating stories. This is based on my assumption, borne of experience, that opposing messages are never random. They are told because they serve a purpose—to challenge the organization's identity claims. The scope of the purpose can range from a desire to see the organization cease to exist to only wishing to make things difficult for the target organization (e.g., limit options or render actions ineffective). The purpose represents the conflict or competitive tension that opponents have with the organization, and the messages spread because the tension is recognized and deemed important and interesting by other audiences. Thus, the opposing narrative is that *something about the organization is disagreeable, such that it must change.* For the organization, constructing this narrative involves identifying: (1) the tensions with the organization's narrative, (2) what drives opponents to aggravate this tension, and (3) what their desired outcome is.

Opposing stories of this form are *counternarratives.* *Counternarratives* are narratives that exist primarily to "refute other narratives."[56] They often emerge as "stories ... which offer resistance, either implicitly or explicitly, to dominant cultural narratives."[57] They can emerge from something the organization

---

[56] Philip Samuels, *Fahrenheit 9/11: A Case Study in Counternarrative*, doctoral dissertation (University of Kansas, 2007), 24.

[57] Molly Andrews, "Introduction," in Michael Bamberg and Molly Andrews (Eds.), *Considering Counter-Narratives: Narrating, Resisting, Making Sense* (Amsterdam: John Benjamins, 2004), 1.

said or did, can be fabricated, or can represent disagreement with the organization even existing. Effective counternarratives allow opponents to continuously generate distinct messages that highlight the conflict or tension, such that can be difficult to predict and they reliably raise questions in the minds of other audiences — without necessarily answering those questions. In fact, it is the lack of definitive answers that keep counternarratives interesting and even when the organization is successful in refuting opposing messages. Counternarratives help keep the pressure on the target organization consistent, despite shifting the focus of its messages — such as from words to actions and back.

This chapter discusses where counternarratives come from and how they can be derived from words and actions perceived from the environment. With this knowledge, leaders can develop *defensive narratives*, narratives designed specifically to protect the organization.[58]

WHAT ARE COUNTERNARRATIVES?

Counternarratives are themselves narratives – they are fully-formed stories that exist to refute other narratives. They provide the meaning for which individuals and other organizations can launch attack after attack against an organization until it fails to sustain its competitive advantage through loss of reputation or fracturing of relationships with stakeholders.

One critical quality of counternarratives--*they are never defeated*. Defeating a counternarrative would mean that the story is both eradicated and impossible to re-form in the future. In effect, joint doctrine treats counternarratives just so. Like enemies to be vanquished, counternarratives are to be supplanted by the friendly narrative. But this is not possible. Competition in the strategic environment means that the mere existence of an organization is enough for opposition to emerge. The counternarrative always exists and has the potential to re-surface at any time, especially when conditions are favorable. Therefore, the more feasible and suitable goal is to isolate counternarratives

---

[58] Thomas P. Galvin, *Rethinking Narratives of 'Offence' and 'Defence': Modeling Relationships Among Actors in a Strategic Communication Environment*, faculty paper (Carlisle, PA: Department of Command, Leadership, and Management, 2017).

from the global discourse. *Isolation* means four things – that (a) the organization successfully defends its narrative against the counternarrative and, (b) successful discredits the counternarrative so that, (c) adversaries and other actors cease to use it, or (d) actors who do use it assume unacceptable risk in doing so (e.g., themselves becoming easy targets for criticism).

But are counternarratives strictly adversarial? No. Organizations use counternarratives against friendly organizations when they disagree or have competing priorities. The purpose may be benign, but the existence of conflict and a desire to change the friendly organization's hearts and minds are still present. For example, the U.S. Army's narrative includes claims of excellence in conventional warfare as part of its central character. Although the Army does not disavow the need for counterinsurgency capabilities, calls by national leaders to require the Army to acquire them stem from counternarratives against the Army's identity, suggesting that the Army should change into a more full-spectrum force or dispense with conventional warfare altogether.[59]

Counternarratives can also reflect differences in priority. While clearly on the same national 'team', military organizations and Congressional stakeholders are continuously engaged in discussions over what capabilities and resources the military needs. The differing views reflect different priorities or agendas, different reads on which threats are more salient, and different views on how military spending compares with other government spending. As cooperative as the relationship normally is, the military routinely confronts Congressional counternarratives that drive decisions to change the military to something it does not wish to become.

If an organization has properly identified its own narrative, it is possible to generate a set of likely counternarratives, each based on some predictable tension that causes others to disagree with the organization's words, actions, or existence. The following

---

[59] Numerous military scholars have discussed the challenges of sustaining counterinsurgency capabilities with more deeply-rooted preferences for conventional capabilities. An exemplar is Steven Metz, *Learning from Iraq: Counterinsurgency in American Strategy* (Carlisle, PA: Strategic Studies Institute, January 2007).

represent different ways of thinking about counternarratives and their impacts on the organization:

- *Discrepant Claims Against the Narrative* – Take elements of the organization's narrative that others oppose or criticize, change them, and fashion a story around the changes. These stories leverage known say-do gaps, inconsistencies, and past errors and mistakes. For example, a counternarrative against the Army's professionalism campaign is its being overcome by bureaucracy. The counternarrative claims that the Army therefore tolerates unprofessional behaviors.[60]

- *Repudiation of the Organization's Existence* – These stories emerge from beliefs that the organization exists for nefarious or hidden purposes, essentially disregarding the target organization's narrative utterly. Or, the counternarrative suggests that the world would be better off if the organization did not exist. For example, the announcement of U.S. Africa Command (USAFRICOM) was heavily criticized because of misperceptions surrounding the command's purpose and reasons for its creation.[61] The essence of the counternarrative was that USAFRICOM was a bad idea, should never have been created, and the only acceptable option is to get rid of it.

- *Discrepant Claims by Association* – Organizations sometimes inherit counternarratives aimed at a parent organization or industry, a similar organization elsewhere, or some other entity with whom the organization has ties. For example, some criticisms directed at the U.S. military are actually targeting the U.S. as a whole. In 2007, the announcement of U.S. Africa Command was greeted with criticism that, regardless of the stated purpose, its creation was an attempt at U.S. neocolonialism.[62] The counternarrative

---

[60] Don M. Snider, *The Army's Campaign Against Sexual Violence: Dealing with the Careerist Bystanders* (Carlisle, PA: Strategic Studies Institute, July 2013).

[61] Edward Marks, "Why USAFRICOM?" *Joint Force Quarterly* 52 (1st Quarter 2009): 148-151.

[62] David E. Brown, *AFRICOM at 5 Years: The Maturation of a New U.S. Combatant Command* (Carlisle, PA: Strategic Studies Institute, August 2013).

was against the nation; the command was a convenient target.

- *Post-Crisis Fall-out* – These often follow scandal or crises from which adversaries (perhaps including victims, witnesses, and their followers) emerge fearing or expecting the scandal or crisis to repeat or claiming that conditions leading to the crisis are still unchanged. Such stories present the crisis as indicators of systemic flaws or uncorrected attitudes among members. Examples include the counternarratives against the U.S. military related to recurrent sexual harassment and assault problems, as victims and their advocates criticized the poor handling of cases, perceived lax enforcement, and retribution against victims.[63]

Sometimes, opponents will be open and explicit about the tension and desire for change. This was certainly the case with U.S. Africa Command. But other opponents may prefer to keep the counternarrative hidden, deliberately passing messages that attack the organization while hiding their underlying purpose. This ostensibly provides opponents with protection from counterattack and freedom to generate new opposing messages as others cease to be effective. The target organization must therefore derive the counternarrative from messages in the environment, not always an easy task.

How can one trace opposing messages back to a counternarrative?

Counternarratives are difficult to trace with precision because the messages stemming from them are dynamic. The actual counternarrative resides in the mind of the opponent, and it changes and evolves as the opponent learns which messages work, which do not, and which risk exposing the opponent to criticism. The messages can also change in tone based on the audience—an adversary may use more aggressive language, whereas a concerned friend using the same counternarrative may

---

[63] Molly O'Toole, "Retaliation Against Victims of Military Sexual Assault Still Persists," *DefenseOne*, December 4, 2014, http://www.defenseone.com/business/2014/12/retaliation-against-victims-military-sexual-assault-still-persists/100536/ (accessed 22 June 2016).

express the disagreement more politely. Different messages and tone, but rooted in the same counternarrative.

The first step is to strip away the tone of the message and examine the message itself. *Tone* is the character of how the message is delivered, the extent of emotion or ration conveyed by the speaker or doer toward the recipient.[64] By setting aside the tone, it is easier to ask *what exactly is being targeted*? Speakers set tone through word choice, manners of emphasis, expressions conveying empathy, reading difficulty, and use of neutral language.[65] Speakers also set tone nonverbally through body language and demeanor as they speak to an audience.[66] Opponents can use tone as a tool to intentionally distract the target. For example, offensive language could be useful for causing a sensible target to be less able or less willing to respond, thereby weakening the rebuttal. Or, opponents can build messages around exhaustively rational arguments with excessive data and logic. Such messages can overwhelm the target who may feel the need to analyze the argument before being comfortable responding.

As leaders analyze the messages, common themes should appear around the three parts of the story – nature of the conflict, its intensity, and what changes that the opponents desire. From these, leaders can fashion a draft counternarrative that can help them predict other opposing messages that opponents might later use. In the USAFRICOM case, once leaders determined that opponents shared a common counternarrative that the new command represented American neo-colonialism, it was easy to guess how opponents would question and challenge USAFRICOM's activities as they occurred. Armed with that

---

[64] Jennifer Lombardo, "Understanding the Tone and Voice of Your Message," *study.com*, https://study.com/academy/lesson/understanding-the-tone-and-voice-of-your-message.html (accessed 19 April 2018).

[65] Dana Lynn Driscoll, "Tone in Business Writing," April 21, 2010, *Purdue Online Writing Lab*, https://owl.english.purdue.edu/owl/resource/652/1/ (accessed 19 April 2018).

[66] Jeff Thompson, "Is Nonverbal Communication a Numbers Game?" *Psychology Today*, September 30, 2011, https://www.psychologytoday.com/us/blog/beyond-words/201109/is-nonverbal-communication-numbers-game (accessed 19 April 2018).

knowledge, USAFRICOM leaders routinely pre-empted those opposing messages as it promoted its activities.[67]

Organizations will likely face multiple counternarratives, and leaders may decide to prioritize them according to effectiveness against the organization's standing campaign. Effectiveness is based on how much of the organization's narrative is refuted, the ease of which opposing messages spread among audiences, and how much more credence given to them over the organization's own message (more details will be given in the next Chapter on audience analysis). The greatest threats would likely target all three components of the organizational identity (central character, distinctiveness, temporal continuity) and be presented in adversarial form with no gaps – i.e., it is a very thorough, rational, and reasonable criticism or attack against the organization's narrative. Counternarratives that are more emotional in character and rely on inflamed rhetoric to gather attention are less likely to be effective, as over time inconsistencies will come to light between the target organization's narrative and the construed image of the organization assumed in the counternarrative. Using the USAFRICOM example, the counternarrative of U.S. neo-colonialism held by African opponents was based on conjecture, not fact. This became apparent as opponents attempted without success to re-characterize USAFRICOM's activities based on a false belief that these programs were secretly hiding nefarious U.S. intentions. Audiences soon ceased to believe the opponents.[68]

CAN ORGANIZATIONS DEFEND THEMSELVES?

Seeing counternarratives as communicating on the offense – in a team sport sense – allows one to think in terms of a corresponding defense. Unfortunately, the communication literature has historically been unkind to matters of defense. A seminal article on defensive communication conflates it with emotional defensiveness, which is considered undesirable.[69] The remedy is a climate of greater openness, empathy, trust, and

---

[67] Galvin, *Two Case Studies*.

[68] Ibid.

[69] Glen H. Stamp, Anita L. Vangelisti, and John A. Daly, "The Creation of Defensiveness in Social Interaction," *Communication Quarterly* 40, no. 2 (1992): 177-190.

avoiding premature judgment.[70] Put another way, defense and defensiveness are like an adversarial narrative to be conquered by the proper open climate.[71] But most recent scholarship challenges this notion that defensiveness is undesirable.[72] What if the relationship between actors in the environment includes past violations of trust of the other party, adversarial relationships, differences in status and power, and the consequences of the issue at hand?

How does an organization defend itself against a counternarrative? Put another way, how does one construct a story that counters the counternarrative and protects the organization's own narrative from harm?

Defensive narratives serve this role, defending the narrative from harm. They provide the ways and means by which organizations can generate responses to criticisms much the way opponents generate criticism against the organization. They also shield organizational members, giving them emotional and cognitive space to regroup and re-establish faith and confidence in their own narratives. Defensive narratives are themselves counternarratives. They counter another's counternarrative. Thus, a suitable alternative name is *counter-counternarrative* or C-CN. I will use this acronym hereafter.

C-CNs can assume any combination of three characters: (1) refuting, (2) mitigating, and (3) accommodating counternarratives. When organizations defend by *refutation*, they essentially issue messages containing discrepant claims against the counternarrative. In other words, *your counternarrative is wrong* and therefore audiences should not believe or share it. *Wrong* can mean factually or perceptually wrong (e.g., audience is misinformed) or misleading (e.g., audience is disinformed or duped). The C-CN thus negates the opposing message and

---

70 Jack R. Gibb, "Defensive Communication," *Journal of Communication* 11, no. 3, (September 1961), pp. 141-148. This statement characterizes a *supportive climate* as the opposite of a *defensive climate*.

71 For example, Kathy Garvin-Doxas and Lecia J. Barker, "Communication in Computer Science Classrooms: Understanding Defensive Climates as a Means of Creating Supportive Behaviors," *ACM Journal of Educational Resources in Computing* 4, no. 1 (March 2004): 1-18.

72 Stamp, Vangelisti, and Daly, "Creation of Defensiveness," 187-188.

provides the organization with opportunities to set the record straight and promote their own narrative.

Refutation as a strategy can be risky for the organization, however. Taken to an extreme, refutation C-CNs can make the organization appear confrontational. More than the other forms of C-CN, a refutation C-CN easily moves to a counternarrative launched against the opponent – *your counternarrative is wrong* becomes *you are wrong*.

Defense by *mitigation* lessens the impact of an opposing message by deflecting it, ignoring it, or reducing its importance. It repudiates the counternarrative's existence, sending signals to opponents that *your counternarrative is irrelevant.*[73] This form of defense generally avoids acknowledging and addressing the content of the opposing message. Instead, the opposing messages' existence is distracting and diverts energy away from the organization's preferred communication. Like refutation, this form of defense can be risky if overused as it causes the organization to appear evasive, arrogant, or condescending. Rather than shutting down communication, they can cause opponents to launch messages charging the organization with not listening, inflexibility (e.g., staying 'on message' regardless of the circumstances), or lacking empathy.

Accommodation produces the most engaging C-CNs, designed as partial acceptance of the opposing message. The defense comes in the form of a phrase beginning with *but* — *we agree with your counternarrative on these points, but not those others.* Accommodation C-CNs convey empathy for audiences while sustaining the organization's own autonomy to incorporate the points of agreement at times, places, or conditions of the organization's choosing. In essence, the purpose is to maintain freedom of maneuver while ceding part of the argument. Thus, accommodation C-CNs resemble negotiable positions. Unlike the other two forms of C-CNs, the desired outcome of the communication is less certain. So, messages from the C-CN may

---

[73] A metaphor I sometimes use for mitigation C-CNs is *talk to the hand,* an idiom from the 1990s that represented an openly-expressed desire by the receiver (the organization in this case) to not listen to the sender (the opponent).

include those that refute or mitigate the disagreeable points of the counternarrative.

Risks of accommodation are many, so leaders must use such strategies carefully. The organization may be seen as too pliable or leaders indecisive in the face of opposition. Compromise, or even openness to it, may be seen as weakness on the part of the leader or signal a leader's willingness to unilaterally undo the organization's narrative.

An implication for leaders is how closely coupled are the organization's promotion of its narrative and its use of defensive narratives. One expects that professional organizations such as the military will keep them closely coupled, such as defensive messages would avoid contradicting the narrative. However, some organizations may choose a looser form of coupling and exercising defensiveness in hopes of shutting down communication, even if the organization's statements conflict with its narrative.

SUMMARY AND IMPLICATIONS

Organizations devote a lot of energy competitively communicating. As shown in this Chapter, they face a barrage of opposing messages, but through carefully analysis they may derive a root story—the counternarrative—from which these messages emerge. From this, they can defend themselves from through consistent application of C-CNs.

The challenge is that counternarratives are never defeated. Instead, they merely go quiet. Thus, while leaders may express a desire to eradicate false information from the environment, it is pragmatically impossible to do so. The more realistic goal of a standing campaign is to deny opportunities for counternarratives to spread. In other words, *isolate the counternarrative*. This is a containment strategy—keeping the counternarrative confined to only those actors whose minds cannot be changed and convincing as many other actors as possible to reject or repudiate it.

The fact that counternarratives can never be defeated is naturally frustrating to leaders accustomed to defeating other kinds of adversarial entities, like enemy forces. It can feel like a never-ending defensive stand against resurfacing messages by actors without prior interest or opinion of the organization. Worse, counternarratives could be spread or shared by friendly actors if they have cause to believe it or at least not immediately reject it. Thus, defending the organization's narrative may involve influencing friendly actors and stakeholders. Counternarratives can also persist even when no one shares them, because memories are long and an organization's mistakes or flaws may recur. After years or even decades of silence, a mistake can rekindle old criticisms and fuel new ones. Today's media environment enables this because the Internet and social media do not purge outdated and incorrect information. Opponents can easily draw from whatever information suits their preferred counternarratives and fabricate plausible stories against organizations. Audiences who fail to cast critical eyes on these messages fall prey to them and may share them unwittingly because of the emotions felt.

Consequently, while traditional communication literature focuses more on combatting adversarial actors, *the greater threats to the organization's narrative are actually the counternarratives they face.* This is especially true if the source of a counternarrative is a stakeholder. As will be seen in the next Chapter, an organization's stakeholder may not agree with the organization's narrative and may desire to change the organization in ways that the organization's leaders do not wish. This can become very challenging for the leaders who must balance their roles as stewards of their organizations' narratives with their responsibilities to satisfy their stakeholders.

CHAPTER 4. WHO ARE THE AUDIENCES?

The term *audience* is vague. Any categorization will work, so long as it represent a collection of individuals who share something in common and thus represent a unified collective of people that an organization wants to deliver messages to. Other organizations, families, social groups, assemblies, random bystanders—all these can be audiences if they are capable of receiving a communication.

When senior leaders conduct campaigns, they often have particular audiences in mind to whom they wish to deliver messages. They may be formal organizations such as other federal or state government agencies, private sector businesses, or partner militaries. They may be particular social groups (e.g., ethnic groups, local civil leaders) or professionals (e.g., engineers, scientists). They may also be internal, such as groups of members (e.g., officers, noncommissioned officers, enlisted, civilians) and others of importance (e.g., contractors, family members and other dependents).

It would be simple if people could be characterized or bucketed into exactly one of these groupings, but of course this is not possible. How people self-identify depends on the situation and often differs from the organizational leader's perspective. Individuals can be members of multiple audiences, and their relationships with each can conflict. Also, in today's information environment, people are more empowered to see themselves as audiences of one. They prefer either direct contact or to receive information from those they follow on news or social media, rather than groupings established by the senders.

There are two important implications, including one that violates an old rule about strategic communication. First, leaders would prefer a stable and durable set of audiences to communicate with, but the environment says otherwise. Audiences are dynamic and numerous, and it takes greater energy to reach them all than in times past. As leaders do not have infinite reserves of energy to communicate with all audiences equally, they must pick and choose who to speak to and what to say, and set conditions that allow their messages to spread.

The second implication is that *tailoring to the audience* is not as useful a strategy as before. One a staple of oral and written communication skills classes, tailoring can be dangerous when the message is nuanced or sensitive. What is told to one group is now expected to be broadcast worldwide. Those who tailor their messaging too much may incur gaps among their own messages, putting their credibility at greater risk.

I believe the better approach is to model the relationships leaders have with audiences and determine how communication enhances or changes those relationships in ways beneficial to the organization. Thus, this chapter describes how to identify audiences for any campaign based on three key factors — *scope, composition*, and *relationship* with the organization.[74]

What is an *Audience*?

A *communication campaign audience* (hereafter in this book 'audience') is *a socially constructed collective presumed to read, watch, or listen to the campaign's intended messages in a generally consistent way based on common identity factors relevant to the campaign's goals.*[75] The operative phrase is socially constructed, and the perspectives of senders and receivers of messages may differ. A military officer delivering a speech to community leaders may think of the leaders as a single homogeneous audience, and therefore sends messages relevant for the whole. However, the community leaders may be splintered between supporters and opponents of the military, among rival political parties or groups, or mixed on whether the speech touches on an important or unimportant topic. In this case, the officer sees one audience while the audiences sees two or more.

Some audiences can be dynamic, forming and breaking up according to the situation. Consider how audiences may coalesce in times of crisis. In ordinary times there may be many different groups with separate agendas and relationships with the organization, sharing little in common with each other. As the crisis unfolds, these groups may coalesce and act as a much larger

---

74 Galvin, *Two Case Studies*, Chapter 5.
75 Based on Richard Halloran, "Strategic Communication," *Parameters*, Vol. 37, No. 3 (Autumn 2007), 8.

whole—all interested in what the organization will do about the crisis. What were many audiences suddenly becomes one large one, from both sender and receiver perspectives. Other audiences can be seen as more stable, particularly when the audience is an organization whose overall identity and structure changes little over time, but can also include any other collective where the identity is less mutable, such as demographic groups (e.g., gender, race, ethnicity, disability, etc.) where individuals generally self-identify as audience members regardless of circumstance.

For standing campaigns, the typical organization has a cadre of stable audiences that they routinely communicate with. These may include: (1) stakeholders who hold positions of power or authority over the organization, (2) direct customers or clients of the organization's goods and services, (3) potential customers and clients with whom the organization wishes to reach, (4) competitors of the organization who may be cooperative under certain circumstances and adversarial in others, (5) the general public who may or may not hold opinions of the organization, and (6) the members of the organization itself, who may hold interest in the strategic direction the organization's leaders take. Anything the organization does or decides to do will likely require engagement with, and possibly permission from, audiences within this cadre. Named campaigns often involve many of these same audiences. Even when the topic of the campaign is not salient to the audience, it may wish to exercise power and influence over the named campaign anyhow to reinforce the relationship with the organization.

Understanding the relationships that the organization has with its audiences is critical for named campaigns, as the topic of the campaign may turn friend into foe, foe into ally against a common opponent, or push a fence-sitter off the fence. Leaders will naturally desire for all audiences to be friendly, but it is unrealistic to expect a campaign to change all the minds within such diverse collections of people. A more realistic outcome is that, in general, audiences do not rebel against the organization and take no specific actions to inhibit campaign goals. At the same time, leaders modify those relationships critical to achieving the campaign goals.

How does one differentiate one audience from another?

Because audiences are dynamic, leaders must make a best guess as how audiences define themselves, and how strongly committed they are to the presumed collective identity. For campaign purposes, it is better to consolidate audiences if possible. This allows leaders to develop fewer messages and simplify campaigns. Plus, there is lower risk of inconsistency when leaders tailor messages for delivery at specific events. However, the campaign determines how audiences are differentiated. For example, some service recruiting campaigns may be targeting the population at large while others aim for specific groups based on the needs of the service. Thus, it is important for campaigners to establish how one campaign defines its audiences such that other campaigns are not unduly constrained.

Audience scope is therefore more than just how big an audience is. It also addresses the logic associated with how the boundaries are drawn. The audiences of the organization's standing campaign should be stable, broad, and clearly differentiated, reflecting the organization's enduring relationships in the environment. Named campaigns will therefore vary, but should mainly involve narrower target audiences that are subgroups from an audience of a standing campaign. Back to the recruiting campaign example, the service has the American public as a general audience, but specific recruiting campaigns, e.g., building the military cyber community, focus on recruiting from particular sectors of the public, e.g. high school students with exceptional science and technological skills. Below are two ways that a campaign can define the scope of audience.

The first is *hierarchical* – whether to treat a larger collective whole as a single audience or must its subdivisions be treated as separate audiences. When should a campaign treat an entire industry as one audience, or instead view each company within that industry as separate audiences? How about an entire organization or subdivisions within it? When should a broad class of people identified through demography, geography, familial relationship, or other general category be considered a single audience? With the U.S. military, a common tension is the joint-service boundary, whereby for some campaigns the military is a single audience while for others service identities are more salient.

The second is *representational*, as a large audience may rely on a proxy element or group to represent its interests. For example, about one-third of all federal workers belong to a union.[76] Thus, a campaign may either have the federal workforce as an audience, or may have the union organization as the main audience under the presumption that the workforce will follow the unions' positions. Similarly, the interests of demographic groups may be represented by named groups who communicate on behalf of the large populace. The strength of the relationship of group to those represented is important. Stronger relationships lead to congruence of perspectives and commitments to common messages. Weaker relationships may find the representative group out of step with its own populace, such that the campaign should treat them as two separate audiences.

HOW ARE AUDIENCES COMPOSED?

The purpose for setting the scope is to foster the efficient crafting and delivery of messages. Fewer audiences mean fewer messages to craft. But this necessarily makes some audiences very large and probably widely distributed. It is not possible to reach all members of these audiences equally. Thus, there is a tension concerning the extent to which communicating with a certain part of the audience counts as addressing the entire audience?

Examples in national politics include political candidates or office holders conducting town hall meetings to ostensibly meet with a representative sample of a nation-wide demographic group or to meet with 'leaders' within an industry to represent engaging all firms and businesses within the industry. An assumption is that the more homogeneous the audience, the more likely that the message will be uniformly received and passed on in like fashion to others within the same audience. A second assumption is that certain members within the audience are more important or are more representative than other members. Perhaps they are formal leaders, respected experts or specially

---

[76] U.S. Bureau of Labor Statistics, "Economic New Release," January 19, 2018, https://www.bls.gov/news.release/union2.nr0.htm (accessed 16 April 2018).

entrusted individuals whose opinions may shape those other audience members or who are capable of speaking on other members' behalf.

The second assumption leads to the identification of two different ways that an audience could be composed: (a) an *organizational audience* whereby communications with the audience's leaders or representatives approximate engagement with the audience as a whole, or (b) a *mass audience,* where the audience is composed mainly of autonomous individuals, such that the audience is less likely to have or employ leaders or representatives. In other words, engaging with a mass audience means engaging with greater numbers of its members and not assuming the message is necessarily shared among them.

Some collectives may simultaneously produce both types of audience in a campaign. Examples from the USAFRICOM case[77] are African nations and the peoples of those nations. Messages to the government followed traditional bi-lateral or multi-lateral channels and involved developing, planning, or implementing programs. Messages to the African people stemmed from U.S. and African media and focused on explaining the nature and character of the command. The success of communicating to these audiences depended in part on relationships. USAFRICOM's messages to the people could be undermined by contradicting messages from the governments, for example. Similarly, military campaigns involving family support often involves units as an organizational audience who might help disseminate formal messages, while the campaign also considers all the individual service members as a separate mass audience.

These two types of audience compositions are addressed in more detail below.

Organizational Audiences

The *organizational audience* is the simpler category – when the audience is itself an organization or a well-defined collection, such as an industry. What defines the organizational audience from the mass audience are two things: (1) the presumption of a

---

[77] Galvin, *Two Case Studies*, Chapter 3.

decision-making body that exercises power over the organization and its members, and (2) that the desired outcome is organization level and not individual level.

Formal authorities and communication channels exist such that engagement with the decision-making body (or its representatives, however defined) constitutes engagement with the whole organization, regardless of the views of its members. If the power in the organization is highly centralized, this simplifies engagement with that organization. If power is more diffuse, the campaign may have to engage more widely among organizational leaders to have successfully engaged with the whole, but the campaign audience is still the organization and not the individual.

Consider the example of Congress, specifically committees responsible for oversight or budgeting of the military. Power relationships among committee members is diffuse and each Member is an independent actor, but the committee Chair has additional authorities and responsibilities such as setting the committee agenda and deciding which legislation will be considered for review and passage.[78] Therefore, a campaign would likely have the Committee as the audience and engagement objectives would include engaging the Chair for the purposes of getting particular legislation on the Committee agenda, beyond which the organization would engage individual Members on their questions on the matter. The desired outcome, that the Committee favors the legislation and allows it to move forward, is an organization-level outcome. That not all Members may support the outcome is not germane for the campaign.

"Mass" Audiences[79] (of Individuals)

Strategic communication literature commonly uses the term *mass audience* to represent large collections of people considered

---

[78] Stevens Berry, "What are the Roles of Committee Chairs in the House and the Senate?" *Quora*, August 13, 2014, https://www.quora.com/What-are-the-roles-of-committee-chairs-in-the-House-and-the-Senate (accessed 20 February 2018), and U.S. Senate, "About the Senate Committee System," *U.S. Senate.gov*, http://www.senate.gov/general/common/generic/about_committees.htm (accessed 20 February 2018).

[79] This distinction is drawn from The White House, *U.S. National Strategy for Public Diplomacy and Strategic Communication* (Washington, DC: The White House, 2007), 4-5.

to have important interests in the organization's message.[80] Mass audiences are usually associated with the receivership of forms of *mass communication*, such as radio and television,[81] employed to reach large collections of people.

Mass audiences are collections of individuals grouped together, but not necessarily defined by, a factor such as demographics (e.g., defined by age, ethnicity, nation, gender, etc.), vocations (e.g., the 'media,' 'academia,' 'defense industries'), or communities (e.g., family support groups, church organizations, veterans organizations). Although there may be an organizing body for a mass audience, the body holds little or no authorities or responsibilities over individuals. For example, a church organization is led by a religious leader who has authority over and responsibility for a congregation (or equivalent), but except for matters of a religion nature (which may make the church an organizational audience), variation of individual perspectives is important and there is no organizational-level outcome.

Instead, campaigns weigh outcomes at the individual level of analysis. Individual members of a mass audience may choose to receive the message or not, and may independently decide when or how to engage with the organization. For example, consider a typical town hall meeting that may only have scant participation among citizens content with second-hand information. When taking up a hotly contested or controversial measure however, direct participation may spike as the individual citizens would prefer first-hand receipt of the message vice second- or third-hand. Yet the citizenry is still one mass audience as the campaign treats all individual citizens as equals, and exercises ways and means (including mass media) to the distribute the message to the greatest number of citizens. On the other hand, the organizing body relative to a mass audience may serve as a separate organizational audience. Using the aforementioned examples of representational groups, the representational group is an organizational audience, while the represented populace is a mass

[80] TF on Strategic Communication and Ibid. both use the term but do not define it.
[81] Denis McQuail, Mass Communication Theory: An Introduction (London: Sage, 1983).

audience. For campaigns when the group and populace are unified, leaders should treat it as an organizational audience.

Because of the loose structure and broad scope of mass audiences, campaigns may develop formal rules and protocols to normalize engagements with them. For example, the military has codified public affairs policies regarding senior leader engagement with 'the media,' a mass audience. At a base or command level, senior leaders enact these policies in standing relationships with a stable but dynamic *cadre* of media outlets focused on that base or command (e.g., local television, radio, social media, and individual journalists).[82] Routine engagements might not go beyond this cadre, whereas the communication stays local or otherwise generates limited interest among the broader 'global media.' The relationships allow a common vocabulary and understanding to emerge which aids the leader's communication (e.g., context is understood, leader misstatements caught and corrected without incident). Although the composition of the cadre will change as individual members of the media come and go and leaders move on to other assignments, the relationship remains stable. Under ordinary conditions, the senior leader in that duty position views the cadre as 'the media.'

However, other circumstances can change the composition of 'the media', whether a local crisis or sudden interest in a matter unrelated to the leader (e.g., a study released that negatively reflects on the military, calls for a base realignment and closure (BRAC), a sudden adjustment in the force protection level). 'The media' quickly grows with a greater number of outlets (e.g., national, international, global) seeking direct engagement or closer indirect engagement through the cadre. The audience, 'the media,' is technically unchanged, as the same public affairs policies still govern the leader's engagement. What changes is the relationship with that audience, whereby the prior common vocabulary and understanding may no longer suffice. Whereas the cadre may share a common outlook with the leader or overlook his/her minor misstatements, non-cadre 'media' may

---

[82] The use of *cadre* is based on Galvin, *Two Case Studies*, Chapter 3 on the USAFRICOM case where engagement with mass audiences was accomplished heavily through proxies. One example was the African media since USAFRICOM did not necessarily have the capacity or capability to engage with those audiences directly.

not enjoy the same understanding or be as dismissive of any miscommunication.

This dynamic suggests there are two modes under which mass audiences engage in a campaign. One I will call *limited engagement*, whereby roles, rules, protocols, ordinary relationships, and 'cadres' (or well-understood subsets of the audience) are relatively stable.[83] In limited engagement, the cadre suffices for the audience, and the remainder of that audience is either passive or disengaged. The other I will call *full engagement*. The cadre can no longer act as proxy for the whole audience, whose non-cadre members are more likely to seek direct engagement with the organization. Senior leaders may operate under the same rules and protocols, but the greater intensity and diversity of the engagements will affect their roles and relationships, possibly leading to change in (or temporary relief from) some rules and protocols. While the audience does not change in definition when it shifts mode, campaigns should be mindful of what triggers changes in mode and how it affects the propagation of messages.

HOW DOES ONE PRIORITIZE AUDIENCES?

Clearly, not all audiences are equal in importance for a given campaign. Thus, it is important to sort them systematically into priority order. This is a *stakeholder* approach, which prioritizes audiences based on two factors: scope and power-influence. Drawing from the work of Stephen Gerras, a *stakeholder* is a "person, group, or entity that can be affected by or influence an organization's action."[84] The degree of influence in either direction determines the priority, but the organization must ensure the stakeholders are also properly identified.

There are three levels of stakeholders based on scope and nature of their power and influence. *Primary Stakeholders* have significant and legitimate power over the organization. *Secondary*

---

[83] Ibid. The descriptions of limited and full engagement were derived from a combination of the willingness of the audience to engage on a matter, the trust placed in proxies, and the capacity of the organization to communicate. Also see James Lull, *Media, Communication, and Culture* (New York: Columbia University Press, 2000), 117-119 for a discussion of mass audiences and collective option; and

[84] Gerras, *Stakeholder Management Approach*, 1.

Stakeholders have only broad but often issue-dependent power and far less legitimacy. *Interested Third Parties* have only narrowly established power and legitimacy that is very issue-dependent. The term stakeholder will hereafter refer to Primary and Secondary stakeholders combined to distinguish them from Interested Third Parties. Although we will not consider audiences who do not fall into any of these three categories as an audience of the campaign, we cannot simply ignore them.

Primary Stakeholders

Primary Stakeholders have significant, persistent, and broad-based power and legitimacy over the organization, including decision authority (such as legislative or regulatory) and access to resources vital to the organization's mission or critical to sustaining the organization's identity and image.[85] Legitimacy is key; combining it with power over resources and decisions place Primary Stakeholders in substantive positions of authority.[86] This legitimacy drives organizations to engage with Primary Stakeholders in a regulated fashion, with clear rules and protocols.

For the U.S. military, Congress is an example of a Primary Stakeholder. Congress has the legislative power over the military via the federal budget process, and sufficient legitimacy to require defense leaders to testify on call, even military commanders actively engaged in warfighting. The military also has Primary Stakeholders among other national leaders with decision making authority or significant influence over the military such as the President, the Department of State, and the Office of Management and Budget. The National Guard has additional Primary Stakeholders in state governors and other state officials. The power and legitimacy of Primary Stakeholders affects relationships, professional and personal, between senior military leaders and Primary Stakeholder members. Personal relationships must still generally follow protocols (e.g., ethical

---

[85] Ibid. My use of *primary stakeholder* mirrors the upper half of Figure 2 in which Gerras describes audience with "high power" over the organization.

[86] Ronald K. Mitchell, Bradley R. Agle, and Donna J. Wood, "Toward a Theory of Stakeholder Identification and Salience: Defining the Principle of Who and What Really Counts," *The Academy of Management Review* 22, No. 4 (October 1997), 860.

guidelines) delineating personal from professional contacts as means of protecting the legitimacy of the organization-stakeholder relationship.

Primary Stakeholders are *always* organizational audiences, never mass audiences. This is true even when primary stakeholders are single named individuals, because they formally draws power and legitimacy from an office, which is an organization. So, it is the President who, vested by Constitutional authority, serves as Commander-in-Chief over the military — and not "Bill Clinton," "George Bush," or any other individual holding the position since they cede such power and authority when they leave office. The same is also true of Congressional members whose stakeholder authorities end as they leave Congress.

Primary Stakeholders can also be internal to the organization, but they too derive power and legitimacy from the organization. The chains of command and support, for example, collectively constitute an internal Primary Stakeholder audience of near-universal application in the military. These officers and noncommissioned officers ordinarily exercise direction from the military's leadership, and as such possess the formally vested authorities and responsibilities that are distinct and steeped in the tradition that constitutes power and legitimacy over the military. Similarly, inspectors general and staff judges advocate have certain vested powers and legitimacy that explicitly exceed that of the commanders they serve directly, though restricted to certain conditions as established in rules and protocols.

It is not necessarily the case that Primary Stakeholders of the standing campaign will also be Primary for all named campaigns. The stakeholder may not consider the named campaign important and thus may not interfere with it so long as the organization addresses the stakeholder's interests outside the named campaign.

Secondary Stakeholders

Secondary Stakeholders are those with sufficient power and legitimacy to affect the organization, but not with the dominant authority of a Primary Stakeholder. Mass audiences (e.g., the "public") can be a Secondary Stakeholder, and often is for communications campaigns for the military. Hereafter, "Stakeholder" will refer to Secondary Stakeholders, while Primary Stakeholders will always be referred with the 'Primary' moniker.

Absent dominant authorities, some Stakeholder influence over the organization is indirectly through the Primary Stakeholders. This indirect influence is manifested in information flows, negotiation, persuasion, or coercion. The success of such influence depends on their perceived legitimacy on the pertinent matter, which sometimes may require authentication or certification by the campaigning organization. In effect, there is normally a "mutual power-dependence" relationship by which the Stakeholder and the organization need each other in some way.[87] Below are four types of relationships.

Based on Resource Pooling and Capability Development. Mutual dependence can be rooted in the ability to garner resources to accomplish the organization's purpose. The defense industry is such a Stakeholder for the U.S. military, which clearly relies on them for goods and services. In return, industry depends on the military for its business contracts which, in some cases, equates to its entire existence. In essence, both sides depend on each other for the ability to develop and sustain capability. While the defense industry must go through a Primary Stakeholder, such as Congress, to exercise influence over military acquisition decisions, there are routine contacts and information sharing between industry and military officials. Primary Stakeholders (especially Congress) develop or endorse laws and regulations to govern such contacts; examples include rules and protocols such as the Federal Acquisition Regulation and DoD documents governing all contacts between the parties to prevent undue influence, foster fair competition, and prevent unauthorized commitments of federal resources.

Based on a Principal-Agent Relationship. This regards stakeholders who benefit from, and in many ways depend on, the organization's ability to deliver capability. For example, the

---

[87] Ibid., 861.

American public is a Stakeholder and a client of the military's ability to provide for the national defense. In return, the public is a resource pool for potential service members; a source of morale and welfare through civic organizations, host communities, and volunteers among others; a source of information; and a barometer for national attitudes and culture to which the military must stay attuned. The public's interests in military affairs is profound and influence can be very high.[88]

Under ordinary circumstances, the public's influence on the military is similarly indirect as for the defense industry. Rules and protocols exist that govern contacts with the public. The military may respond to, but not automatically act upon, every grievance or issue delivered from an individual member of the public; however the military must respond when a member of the public approaches their representative in Congress and Congress formally forwards the issue to the appropriate military leader. Certainly the military may act independently in response to an issue raised directly by the public, but this only occurs locally or on a small-scale. Large-scale issues typically are the subject of communications with Primary Stakeholders.

The American Public is not the military's only client. US service members often provide training and education directly to foreign units or forces, during which the military serves as a provider and the foreign government is the client even though the Primary Stakeholder governing the transaction for the U.S. is the Department of State. Although some are short-term contacts, the stakeholder relationships between the U.S. and its alliances or coalition partners can be long-term.

Based on a Peer Relationship. An important factor regarding the influence between an organization and a Stakeholder is that the level of influence may differ according to the issue at hand. For example, while the Department of State is a Primary Stakeholder for certain military services provided to foreign militaries, it is a Secondary Stakeholder for military operations conducted in foreign environments. The US conducts many interagency activities with a designated lead authority, but such

---

[88] See Peter Feaver, *Armed Servants: Agency, Oversight, and Civil-Military Relations* (Cambridge, MA: Harvard University Press, 2003).

authorities exist primarily for coordination and synchronization, essentially serving as a leader among peers; the true authority (the Primary Stakeholder) rests at a higher national level. This is an example of a *peer relationship*, whereby the need to pool resources together to accomplish a collective mission drives the mutual dependence, an arrangement necessary for each organization to serve its individual purposes.

Based on Intense, Narrow Interests. Some Stakeholders identify themselves based on narrow interests that are of high importance. Otherwise, they may have no legitimacy whatsoever. Lobbyists or special interest groups may have influence over Congressional members on behalf of their clients to incorporate certain provisions in bills (i.e., retaining specific weapons systems programs), but their interests and social standing does not ordinarily provide them with the same levels of legitimacy on any other issue. Their goals are to ensure the prominence of their interests and to have influence Primary Stakeholders of the organization. They accomplish these goals through the intensity of their messages—high in quantity and provocative in nature such that it draws attention to their cause.

Interested Third Parties[89]

Interested Third Parties can be individuals or organizations. They ordinarily have little or no power or legitimacy in organizational affairs, except for: (a) very specific issues by which they can articulate particular expertise, or (b) the demonstrable ability to disrupt the power and/or legitimacy of the organization or other stakeholders. Neither case assumes a formal or informal relationship with the organization, although such stakeholders within the U.S. are naturally part of the American Public seeking to exercise greater or more direct power and influence.

---

[89] These were included in the category of 'secondary stakeholders' in Max B. E. Clarkson, "A Stakeholder Framework for Analyzing and Evaluating Corporate Social Performance," *The Academy of Management Review*, Vol. 20, No. 1 (Janaury 1995), 107. However, the degree of influence among secondary stakeholders exhibited in Carlson and in Mitchell, Agle, & Wood suggested that a further subdivision to secondary and tertiary ("third party") was warranted.

What differentiates these parties from other audiences is the notion of *claimed legitimacy*[90] by which the organization may take risk if it does not honor the Interested Third Party's claim. Claiming legitimacy alone is insufficient to imbue the third party with legitimacy or power; the organization must at least acknowledge the claim, even if it neither accepts nor abides it.

Specifically, Third Parties (hereafter "Interested" is assumed) can be either sources of counternarratives aimed at disrupting an organization's relationships with key stakeholders or strong (though disinterested) supporters helping to carry forward the organization's narrative (not necessarily with the blessing of the organization). In the former case, because their influence is indirect, Third Parties are difficult for organizations to engage directly using C-CNs. In the latter case, the Third Party might be hijacking an organization's messages to support a counternarrative against somebody else, possibly corrupting the message in the process. Some general categories follow:[91]

Activists and Activist Groups. At the strategic level, political activism has a strong influence over the communications environment. Whether individuals or groups, activists typically disrupt or provoke, often seeking change. As communicators, they act on the offense, largely (maybe exclusively) promoting a counternarrative. Some activist groups exercise a narrative which expresses alternate worldviews and desire radical change in support of it, while others may not have this worldview formulated, in which case the fight is its own reward. While some groups may join a broader, longer-term cause, such as environmental movements, others may arise specifically due to a particular organizational action or decision.

Individual activists can be more focused and quite effective in pushing a counternarrative. However, doing so independently requires sustained energy, meaning individuals must either work to stay in the spotlight or ensure others can further the cause. Examples are celebrities who employ their persona in favor of a particular counternarrative against a nation or organization, such

[90] Clarkson, 106.
[91] These are generalizations of example third party audiences in Galvin, *Two Case Studies*.

as expressing concerns over climate change, human rights, or poverty brought about through questionable policies or actions. Depending on their personal situation, their involvement may be quite temporary; still, their celebrity status can have a high impact on the discourse, and because they tend not to be Primary Stakeholders, they may be unswayed by C-CNs.

Aggrieved Parties. A common basis for counternarrative is that the organization, or something that the organization represents, has committed an actual or perceived wrong. Therefore, the audience presents a counternarrative explaining their grievances and seeking reparations or reconciliation. Such counternarratives have strong emotions attached, fueling sympathy for their cause and placing the organization in a bad light, even when the counternarratives are unjustified.

Passive Supporters. At the strategic level, there are actors who may agree with and support an organization's narrative but must remain neutral or silent for political or other reasons. For many, neutrality is part of the organizational identity and often the primary image they project. If asked or encouraged to express support for the organization, they will decline and, if pushed, will rebel. For them, the appearance of a relationship is inimical to their aims or ability to accomplish their mission. They may even publicly join in criticism against the organization if it permits them operating space, as they could easily pursue counternarratives to preserve their neutrality.

General Proxies (e.g., Academia and Reporters). These actors legitimate phenomena they observe and report, yet are not necessarily subject to the same phenomena. For example, academics use scientific methods to establish rigor in their research, adding credence and acceptability to their reports. Reporters use journalistic methods to objectively pursue a story. Such actors place high value on autonomy, which means that while they may agree with an organization's position on matters, they are sensitive to any appearance of taking sides. These actors can reach audiences the organization cannot, or offer cogent arguments an organization cannot make. As such, they can be a resource to further an organization's narrative. Their autonomy can be a disadvantage however, allowing them (and in many cases requiring them) to pursue and argue both sides of an issue, essentially presenting both narrative and counternarrative together.

How does one assess relationships with an audience?

As leader assemble the list of audiences for a campaign, the associated question is this: *are "they" with us or against us?* Determining one's friends and foes is usually easy, as they either communicate favorably or unfavorably about the organization. Unfortunately, communication campaigns often involve audiences who are neutral – neither friend nor foe, *per se*. About the organization, these audiences can be uninterested or apathetic (e.g., listening politely but little else), ambivalent (e.g., conflicted between two views about the organization), or staunchly resistant (e.g., does not wish to be bothered, has more 'important' things to worry about). Meanwhile, friend and foe can mean many things. Friends can either be active supporters who communicate in unison with the organization, or could be passive — essentially cheerleading the organization on but otherwise not investing in the organization's campaign directly. Foes can range from completely adversarial to ordinary competitors. or gatekeepers who based on their own interests communicate in opposition to the organization.

Complicating matters is the fact that organizations and their leaders may describe relationships as friendlier or more adversarial than they really are. For example, leaders may prefer to describe the audience as friendly even when the audience is actually more ambivalent. Or, if the audience is an adversary, leaders may prefer to publicly negate anything the adversary says or does while avoiding mentioning anything favorable. This may occur under conditions when leaders who show empathy toward adversaries would be perceived by others as weak or indecisive. Leaders must weigh the benefits and risks of portraying relationships differently from actual practice, while also providing themselves with flexibility to re-characterize relationships as conditions change.

Table 1 shows six characteristic relationships among two parties in a communication environment. The determinant is based on two factors.

Table 1. Six Types of Relationships[92]

Dominant Mode of Communication

		Active	Passive
Dominant From of Narrative	**Narrative**	*Constructive.* Parties share much in common. Communication is open and mutually supportive, possibly due to mutual dependence.	*Agreeable.* Parties share much in common, but only communicate when necessary. One party can reach out to the other with limited resistance.
	Counter-narrative	*Adversarial.* The two parties openly attack each others, whether directly or through third parties (e.g. media). They project incompatible images and often avoid reconciliation or negotiation.	*Competitive.* The identifies of the two parties remain incompatible, but communication is not necessarily hostile. Negotiation is possible, but differences in identity are rarely resolved.
	Defensive Narrative	*Defensive.* Both parties depend on each other in some way but must avoid confrontation, and thus are secretive or mask their true intentions. Parties are ambivalent about the relationship.	*Deflective.* The parties would prefer not to communicate directly. Any direct contact is viewed as an exceptional case or

The first factor is the *dominant form of narrative*, defined as which type of narrative generates the majority of messages between the organization and the audience. If the audience is friendly, the narrative would dominate as both sides would communicate their shared understandings with each other to harmonize communications with others. Adversarial audiences use mostly counternarratives, spending much of their communication attacking the organization and vice versa. Meanwhile, organizations and neutral parties will mostly use C-CNs to communicate defensively, avoiding provocation while keeping communication channels open.

The other dimension, *dominant mode of communication*, reflects the tone and intensity of messages between the two parties. Active mode is when the organization and the audience prefer direct or unequivocal communication between them. Direct does not necessarily mean face-to-face, but that the intended recipient of the message is made known. Passive mode is when the organization and the audience prefer indirect communication,

---

[92] Original table developed by author.

sending signals to the other party without calling them out. Passive communication also occurs when communication is one-sided, meaning that one side communicates directly one way, but the other party responds indirectly.

For campaign purposes, once the current relationships are ascertained, the question for leaders is whether or not the campaign must change a particular relationship either as a campaign goal in itself or as catalyst to achieving campaign goals. It is presumed that the campaign's goals include sustaining other relationships at no worse than status quo. In addition to the organization favorably influencing stakeholders, the following constitute four ways of expressing desired changes in relationships.

Isolate Adversaries. Recall that counternarratives are never defeated. Neither too are adversaries, so the goal would be to discredit them and limit their influence over the environment. The adversary will not likely change their minds, but their inability to attack the organization successfully may cause them to become passive or to only communicate with a shrinking number of allies.

Foster Healthy Competition. Competitors and competition can be beneficial to an organization, allowing it to promote its narrative in contrast to the narratives of others. 'Healthy' competition can be described as relationships with a competing audience that emphasizes the contrasts but does not necessarily attack the competitor in the eyes of other audiences. In other words, communication takes the high road. Recruiting campaigns among the services are competitive, for example, as the services vie for the best recruits. Although most of the communication is about promoting the service's own narratives, they enact counternarratives against the other services subtly to make their own service more attractive to potential recruits. Similarly, organizations can also foster competition with stakeholders should they differ on competing visions for the organization.

Win Over Influencers. Rather than pursuing a broad 'winning hearts and minds' goal, the organization changes the minds of specific audiences ("influencers") whose newfound favor or reduced opposition toward the campaign convinces stakeholders to become more favorable. The campaign can do this in a constructive way through negotiation or by using counternarratives to highlight inconsistencies within the influencers' own narrative. The effect can be temporary, so long as the stakeholder perceives the change in the environment enough to take action.

Do No Harm. One must not conflate 'do no harm' with 'do not communicate.' In ths context, doing no harm means ensuring audiences are given every opportunity to be informed without pushing or provoking them toward acceptance of counternarratives. In essence, it is to keep neutral parties neutral and keep friends friendly, in that order, by reducing the chances of an information void, which opponents will gladly fill with counternarratives.

There is an important final implication from the above. Organizations use counternarratives against their friends and stakeholders. They may not wish to, and generally seek alternative, but they have little choice if the friend or stakeholder is not in agreement with the campaign and is postured to disrupt it. Recalling the old adage that disagreement is not disrespect, should an organization face a stakeholder who is an opponent to the campaign, the organization should develop a well-coordinated, thoughtful rebuttal to the stakeholder's view. While the stakeholders may not change their minds, the counternarrative may provide opportunities for dialogue and negotiated solutions. Obviously, using counternarratives is sensitive and can be misperceived as an attack or affront, so exercise caution.

CHAPTER 5. HOW DO WE ORDINARILY COMMUNICATE?

This chapter covers a very complex topic – the internal mechanisms of communicating. Large, complex organizations such as militaries have diverse subcultures and identities, robust globally-distributed formal and informal networks, and hosts of laws, regulations, and norms that influence what is said or done, by whom, when, and where. Messages that make sense at the strategic level may not translate well to the front lines of the organization – whether that's the individual service member performing military tasks or individual staff members negotiating and collaborating with peers in other staffs. Also, messages that make sense to certain communities within the military might not make sense to others. While the combat arms, intelligence, signal, logistics, medical services, and many others are all part of the Army, these communities of practice have their own identities and languages, so the one Army message may be heard and enacted differently among members of these disparate communities.

Unfortunately, the typical approach has been to pursue strategic communication efforts top-down, whereby the leader's message is dictated down the chain of command.[93] In a complex hierarchy, the result was disunity of effort more than unity. Scholar Mari Eder, for example, she noted the growth of "boutique strategic communication organizations" throughout DoD, each with its own operating definition of strategic communication.[94] Other authors agree, and have charged the U.S. with exercising an uncoordinated and dysfunctional effort.[95]

It is because of the common usage of *strategic*, along with the elimination of the term *strategic communication* from joint

---

[93] Department of Defense, *Report of the Defense Science Board: Task Force on Strategic Communication* (Washington, DC: Department of Defense, 2009), 1, http://www.acq.osd.mil/dsb/reports/ADA476331.pdf (retrieved 7 July 2015) (hereafter *TF on Strategic Communication*).

[94] Eder, *Leading the Narrative*, 47.

[95] Bolt, "Strategic Communication in Crisis," and Halloran, "Strategic Communication."

doctrine,[96] that this Primer prefers the term *organizational communication*. Organizational communication encompasses the organization's ordinary communication practices beyond those involving the leader. It includes all formal and informal channels established over time that allows the organization to learn, and leverage how information flows and how messages are interpreted across its subcultures.[97] Synchronizing communication takes more than just top-down pressure (although that is precisely what traditional strategic communication approaches prescribe). It requires additional pressures bottom-up and *middle-out*, meaning from field grade officers and civilian equivalents to both up and down the chains of command and across to other organizations. Middle-out communications are vital in large, complex organizations. They validate, re-state, and reinforce the leader's message in all directions. They generate, propose, and disseminate messages that plug gaps and inconsistencies, allowing the organization to self-correct. However, middle-out communications depends greatly on an organizational identity that promotes learning and autonomous action, as prescribed in the Army's Mission Command philosophy.[98]

If the aim is to have the organization present a unified campaign, it is important to analyze and assess its ordinary organizational communication practices. In this chapter, I discuss how to model an organization's communication posture based on *institution theory*. This will help us understand how the complexities of the organization translate into multiple layers of formal structures and informal habits. One can then leverage this information to construct campaigns that address gaps and inconsistencies, and foster a more unified communication effort.

---

[96] Specifically, in joint operations the term *strategic communication* applies only at the national level, while joint commanders exercise *communication synchronization* in support, but effectively not to initiate national strategic communication on its own. See The Joint Staff, *Joint Planning*, Joint Publication 5-0 (Washington, DC: The Joint Staff, June 2017), II-10. I argue that communication synchronization applied to an organization within the force is an example of a named campaign (see Chapter 1) -- a top-down intervention into how the organization ordinarily communicated in peacetime.

[97] Peter J. Senge, *The Fifth Discipline: The Art and Practice of the Learning Organization*, Revised Ed. (New York: Doubleday, 2006), 221-232 on the "Discipline of Team Learning."

[98] U.S. Department of the Army, *Mission Command*, Army Doctrinal Reference Publication 6-0 (Washington, DC: U.S. Department of the Army, 2012).

HOW CAN WE MODEL COMMUNICATION IN AN ORGANIZATION?

Communication is an *institutional practice*, or more simply *institution*.[99] Institutions are "multifaceted, durable social structures, made up of symbolic elements, social activities, and material resources."[100] They represent ways of understanding activities and behaviors of collective bodies (including organizations), and thinking about how they do and should function.[101] Although durable, institutions are dynamic and undergo a life cycle of being "created, maintained, changed, and [then they] decline."[102] Societal and organizational habits and practices, whether desired or not, carry the qualities of an institution. Thus, for our purposes we will treat institution, habit, and practice as synonymous.[103]

Consider the following examples of institutions in military settings. *Command* is a social structure representing special authorities, responsibilities, and privileges afforded officers serving in designated positions. Along with the formal designations, service members view commanders differently from other leadership positions. The *general staff ("G"-staff) structure* is a codified division of labor within a staff used to ensure common understanding of the functions and responsibilities of each division and branch in a complex staff headquarters. Military organizations deviating from the G-staff structure may face difficulties interfacing with other organizations. *Readiness* is a complex institutional practice about

---

[99] This Primer will use *institutional practice* as a social structure at the transactional level. Later, the term *posture* will reflect communication of the whole organization.

[100] W. Richard Scott, *Institutions and Organizations* (Thousand Oaks, CA: Sage, 2008), 57.

[101] Roy Suddaby, et al., "Organizations and Their Institutional Environments – Brining Meaning, Values, and Culture Back In: Introduction to the Special Research Forum, *Academy of Management Journal*, Vol. 53, No. 6 (2010): 1234-1240. This contrasts with other common uses of the term institution: (1) enduring, important, and special organizations (e.g., "*institutions* of higher learning" or the Army as an "*institution*"), and enduring social structures that fall outside of organizational boundaries (e.g., the *institution* of marriage).

[102] Mary Jo Hatch and Tammar Zilber, "Conversation at the Border Between Organizational Culture Theory and Institution Theory," *Journal of Management Inquiry* 21, no. 1 (2012): 94-97, 95.

[103] To be more precise, Scott describes *institutional logics* as "shared frameworks" guiding organizational behavior, especially emphasizing the normative and cultural-cognitive pillars (Ibid., 225). *Habits* are "usual ways of behaving" while *practices* are things done "customarily" (Merriam-Webster). Both terms convey activities guided by institutional logics enacted in organizational settings.

self-measurement, combining formal quantitative analysis, informal normative assessment, and shared understandings regarding the implications of results.[104]

Institutional practices are comprised of three "pillars"[105] – *regulative, normative,* and *cognitive.* For communication practices, these pillars represent different means of passing information and making decisions. *Regulative* channels are formal, codified, and require compliance. In communication, these represent channels that must be used when communicating for specific purposes. For example, if one wishes to speak with the media, one must employ public affairs because this is required per military regulations. Failure to comply results in sanction.[106] The *normative* pillar guides organizations and its members toward acceptable behavior, such that they feel obligated to follow the norms, even when they circumvent or break the rules.[107] The *cognitive* pillar regards how messages spread on their own from member to member. It reveals shared understandings, common beliefs, and values.[108] As Table 2 shows, these pillars represent different means that can enable leader communication. However, the use of these means should align with members' expectations understanding of the situation. Misalignment can engender resistance to or rejection of the leader's message.

Culturally, military organizations heavily employ the regulative pillar, ostensibly to exercise control over the message and its dissemination. This is congruent with expectations of internal and external audiences. For example, the public, stakeholders, and organizational members expect commanders to speak authoritatively over everything that occurs within their commands, and therefore commanders have resources available to help them with this task. Public affairs staffs manage communications released to the media and public, while

---

[104] Thomas P. Galvin, *Leading Change in Military Organizations: Primer for Senior Leaders,* 1st edition (Carlisle, PA: U.S. Army War College, 2018), 41-43.

[105] Scott, *Institutions and Organizations,* 59.

[106] W. Richard Scott, "Approaching Adulthood: The Maturing of Institutional Theory," *Theory and Society,* Vol. 37, No. 5 (2008): 427-447, 428.

[107] Jennifer Palthe, "Regulative, Normative, and Cognitive Elements of Organizations: Implications for Managing Change," *Management and Organizational Studies,* Vol. 1, No. 2 (2014): 59-66, 61.

[108] Ibid., 61.

legislative affairs does same for communications with Congress. These and other communication tasks and responsibilities are governed in joint and Army publications.

Table 2. Three Pillars of Institution[109]

	Regulative	Normative	Cognitive
Shorthand	"Must do"	"Ought to do"	"Want to do"
Basis	Coercion and compliance	Moral governance	Mimicry
Means	Laws, regulations, organizational structures, formal relationships	Norms and habits, obligations, expectations, certifications	Values, shared understandings, common beliefs, shared logics of action
Examples	Chains of command, public affairs, legislative affairs, staff actions	Workarounds, communities of practice, informal channels, subject matter experts	Casual discussions among members, memes, rumors, urban legends
Leaders may…	Send 'official' messages, set new rules or regulations	Set the example, issue guidance or policy	Leadership by walking around, spreading the 'news'
Members may…	Monitor themselves and other members	Routinize what works	Interpret and making sense
Members may resist by…	Following letter of law, not spirit; avoiding blame or shirking responsibilities	Following spirit of the law, not letter; exercising improper workarounds	Spreading rumors, complaining, undermining leader in the eyes of others

Most communications occur informally using the normative and cognitive pillars. From staff work to exercises and operations, much of what military organizations involves norms, habits, and shared understandings. Staff members employ networks and contacts to help stay informed and gets any work done not

---

[109] Adapted by author from Scott, *Institutions and Organizations*, 60.

requiring direct involvement of the supervisor. Deployments involve preparatory events, operations security requirements, mobilization and de-mobilization, and other activities exercising well-established practices that emerge over time but are not necessarily codified.

The internal challenge for leaders of large complex organizations is the degree to which formal communication reaches all members. Leaders may expect thorough dissemination, however at echelon leader messages compete for salience among members. Messages that make sense and are important strategically may not be salient at mid-level or lower levels. Differences in time horizons, language, context, and interpretation causes the meaning of the message to change as it is passed down the chain of command. While direct communications from leader to members such as mass e-mails or so-called *all-hands*[110] events can help improve dissemination of leader messages, they risk disruption to formal channels and do not necessarily improve the salience of messages as received by members--mass e-mails can too easily wind up in the trash folder and the constantly running rumor mill can easily supplant a one-time leader proclamation. Moreover, if a senior leader's words are not supported by or aligned with organizational activity, members are more likely to reject the message. Thus, if a message requires total dissemination, leaders should consider means other than top-down.

WHAT IS A COMMUNICATION POSTURE?

The above suggests that the leader's communications constitute only a small portion of how organizations communicate within their standing campaigns. However, if one is to assess communication at the institution level, it is important to avoid too narrowly focusing on individual interactions and look at the organization as a whole. Thus, I will introduce a different term that conveys the strategic view. I define an organization's *communication posture* as the institution of communication at the strategic (i.e., whole of organization) level

---

[110] Refers to assemblies involving all members of the organization. These often include a keynote address by the senior leader to describe the current and future situations.

and is directly associated with the standing campaign, whereby *communication practices* will refer to localized habits and structures. A communication posture contains four elements: its *communication mission* or purpose for communicating within the environment, and its *communication structures, processes,* and *culture* describing the institutional practice of communicating – the ways and means available to members.[111]

Communication mission – for what purpose does the organization communicate?

An organization's *communication mission* is its internal purpose for communicating. It incorporates the organization's answers to the following questions: What must the organization communicate to survive and thrive in the environment? How does the organization respond to stimuli in the environment? What are the rules or norms that determine whether the organization promotes or defends its narrative, or targets the narratives of others?

There is an important difference with the organization's stated mission. The stated mission is stable and embedded in the organization's narrative, while the communication mission may be more dynamic and personality dependent. Under leadership that is introverted, thoughtful, and cautious, the communication mission may be about defending the narrative from criticism, and therefore the organization as a whole limits or constrains communication activities. When replaced by new leaders exhibiting the opposite personality, the communication mission may change to a more aggressive and promotional posture. The purpose for communicating becomes getting the word out so the organization is better known by others.

Communication structure, process, and culture

How does the organization operationalize its mission through its institutional practices of communication? *Communication structure* represents the formal channels and methods described under regulative pillar of institutions that the organization and its members must do to communicate. It represents mandatory

---

[111] Based on Scott, *Institutions and Organizations,* 60.

activities such as legally-required reports or clearance procedures for release to the media, and formally designated relationships such as legislative affairs stewarding the organization's communication with Congress.

Answers to the following questions are helpful for analyzing the communication structure. What types of communication are required to flow a specific way according to laws, regulations, or other formal means outside the organization's control? What are those regulations and why were they established? How does the organization benefit or suffer from following the regulations? Or *not* following them? And most importantly, to what extent are the rules followed and what governs shifts from tighter to looser controls? With their reliance on formal methods, military organizations will typically tighten controls during times of crisis or other difficulties, but subsequently either loosen them to restore the *status quo ante* or create further formal structure ostensibly to prevent such crises from occurring again in future.

Communication process follows the normative pillar and represents how the organization expects to communicate in the absence of (or in spite of) formal direction, or how the organization bends the rules to comply with formal requirements while protection its narrative from harm. Communication process encompasses norms involving how the organization: (a) reaches and engages with new audiences, (b) chooses to engage in either two-way dialogue or one-way conversations, (c) characterizes change in the environment, (d) uses static messaging (e.g., staying 'on message') or exercises dynamic and tailored messaging, or (e) communicates rationally or emotionally, among others. Understanding such norms helps leaders anticipate how leader messages evolve as they are disseminated throughout the organization.

Communication culture follows the cognitive pillar and represents the deeply-held assumptions and shared understandings of members—from the top leaders to the most junior. These assumptions may align with the narrative, in which case organizational commitment is strong among members. Or, they may not, which could be a source of gaps and inconsistencies in organizational behavior. Leaders should appreciate that some workplace resistance is natural in organizations and not all members will accept or echo espoused messages from the leadership. Thus, assessing communication culture is about how the members respond to such espoused messages in the general case – acceptance, rejection or skepticism, ambivalence, or other?

Challenges of Assessing the Posture

The communication posture is difficult to assess objectively because the leader is a natural part of it. The leader's mere existence alone is influencing how communication occurs. The leader's words and actions have even greater effects. Analyzing the standing campaign involves assessing how communication ordinarily occurs without specific leader intervention (which as describe in Chapter 1 constitutes a named campaign). The goal is to establish a baseline of organizational action from which the leader can assess change based on a named campaign.

Limiting *intervention* is the key. It means avoiding the exercise of words or actions intended to change the way the organization communicates, while not trying to withdraw from the organization either in an attempt to attain an objective stance. Withdrawal may constitute a leader intervention because the organization may react and change its posture so that the flow of information is not interrupted.

In effect, the leader takes on the role of *participant-observer*, which is to say that the leader observes the communication practice while being a part of it.[112] A full description of participant-observation is beyond the scope of this Primer, but given the limited time available to most leaders, guidelines from the literature are in order:

- If leaders know in advance which aspects of the communication posture are most salient, they should focus in depth on practices most related to those aspects.[113]

- If leaders do not know in advance which aspects are most salient and wish to establish a participative culture, they

---

[112] Barbara B. Kawulich, "Participant Observation as a Data Collection Method," *Forum Qualitative Sozialforschung / Forum: Qualitative Social Research* 6, no. 2, Article 43.
[113] This is analogous to *selective observation* in Ibid.

can integrate personal observation with planned engagements to solicit inputs from key members.[114]

Naturally, the above approaches can be overtaken by events such as crises. However, the organization's ordinary reactions to crises can provide invaluable information about the posture.

How Does One Change the Posture?

Having assessed the communication posture for the standing campaign, leaders can consider how to intervene to improve communication effectiveness and unity of effort as needed. This section addresses two processes from institution theory: (1) creating or changing a practice, and (2) eliminating it. These are analogous to culture change within organizations as both formal and informal aspects of the organization could potentially evolve or transform as a result.

Institutionalization – Creating and Changing

Changing and creating institutional practices is done through *institutionalization*, "processes by which social processes, obligations, or actualities come to take on a rule-like status in social thought and action."[115] Key is that all three pillars are enacted. The act of signing of a new regulation does not necessarily create matching norms nor change minds of members. Rather, what is institutionalized may be different from what the leader intended. Members may create norms (e.g., workarounds) that violate the intent of the new regulation. Members may also retain old habits as a way of addressing gaps and exceptions that the regulation does not handle adequately, or as direct contravention to the new regulation.

Scholars have therefore developed three complementary views of how institutions form depending on which pillar was

---

[114] This is analogous to *participative observation* in Ibid..

[115] John W. Meyer and Brian Rowan, "Institutionalized Organizations: Formal Structure as Myth and Ceremony," *American Journal of Sociology* 83, no. 2 (September 1977): 340-363. This was further elaborated in later works describing institutions as broader isomorphic templates. See Paul J. DiMaggio and Walter W. Powell, "The Iron Cage Revisited: Institutional Isomorphism and Collective Rationality in Organizational Fields," *American Sociological Review* 48, no. 2 (April 1983): 147-160 and Stephen R. Barley and Pamela S. Tolbert, "Institutionalization and Structuration: Studying the Links Between Action and Institution," *Organizational Studies* 18, no. 1 (1997): 93-117.

initially emphasized. Figure 5 shows simplified versions of these three views. On the left is depiction of an institution begun through a regulative process – such as the enactment of a new law or a codified change in an organizational structure. This view suggests that the institution forms through a feedback mechanism, whereby favorable results lead to the development of new norms to leverage those results and the copying of those norms across the organization.

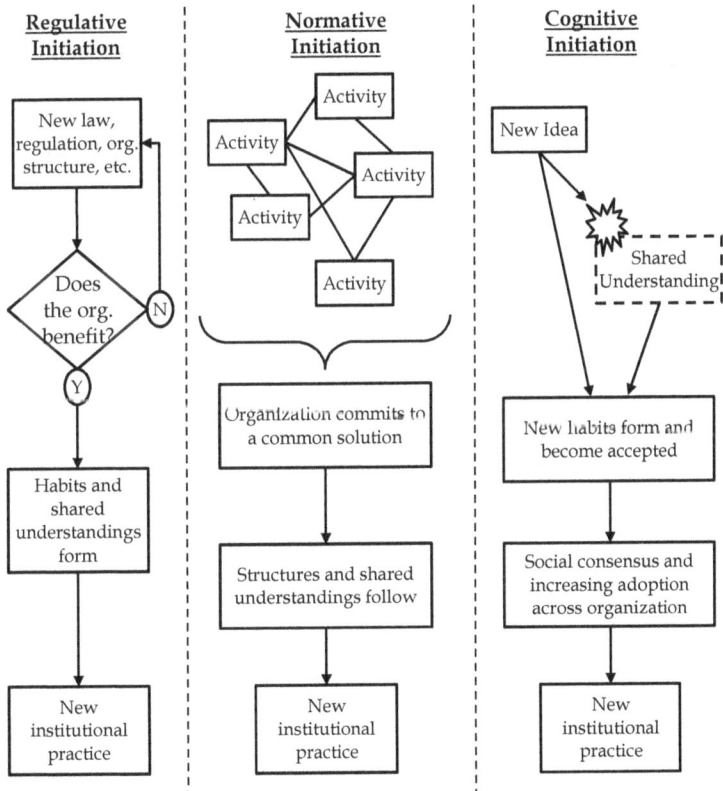

Figure 5. Three ways institutions form[116]

116 Original drawing by author based on Scott, *Institutions and Organizations,* 144-151 which includes an adapted figure cited from Pamela S. Tolbert and Lynne Zucker, "Component Processes of Institutionalization," in *Handbook of Organizational Studies,* eds. Stewart Clegg, Cynthia Hardy, and Walter R. Nord (Thousand Oaks, CA: Sage, 1996), 182.

The center of the Figure depicts normative change. One can describe the graphic as order emerging out of chaos. Different parts of the organization sense a shortcoming or gap and try workarounds or new procedures. These innovations eventually coalesce into common 'best practices' adopted more commonly. The organization then encodes this best practice as the new norm through regulative action while organizational members adopt it as a shared understanding. The organization thus has committed to the formation of a new institution.

Cognitive initiation is at the right side of the Figure, where the institution forms through a change to a shared understanding. A new idea appears that challenges 'conventional wisdom.' The idea may come from new information or stimulus from the environment or a questioning of beliefs in the organization. If the new idea successfully changes minds, then a new habit may form that produces a different shared understanding mimicked across the organization. As consensus builds, new norms and rules may follow.

An important implication is that there are many ways to change an institutional practice. Fixing a broken law does not necessarily require a change to the law, especially if the law is difficult to change. Using normative or cognitive activities may expose weaknesses in the law that foster its change eventually.

De-institutionalization – Withering Away and Stopping

De-institutionalization "refers to the processes by which institutions weaken and disappear."[117] This can be either intentional or through social entropy, "the gradual erosion of [its] taken-for-granted character,"[118] such as practices that cease to have meaning and eventually stop occurring. Institutional scholar Christine Oliver identified several antecedent pressures such as poor organizational performance, conflicting internal interests, competition, social fragmentation, and decreasing historical

---

[117] Scott, *Institutions and Organizations*, 166.
[118] Lynne G. Zucker, "Where do Institutional Patterns Come From? Organizations as Actors in Social Systems" in *Institutional Patterns and Organizations: Culture and Environment*(Cambridge, MA: Ballenger, 1988), 26.

continuity.[119] When these pressures exist, an institutional practice dissipates or becomes rejected by members, creating room for alternative practices to appear, which may replace the old practice.[120] Importantly, outlawing an institutional practice alone does not cause its de-institutionalization; it is the cognition that rejects the practice or allows its dissipation that matters most. Figure 6 depicts several pressures that contribute to an institution being discontinued.

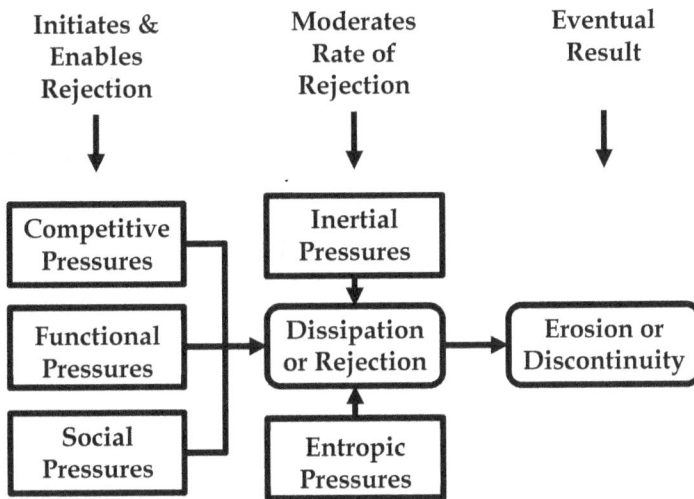

Initiates & Enables Rejection | **Moderates Rate of Rejection** | **Eventual Result**

Competitive Pressures	Inertial Pressures	
Functional Pressures	Dissipation or Rejection	Erosion or Discontinuity
Social Pressures	Entropic Pressures	

Figure 6. How institutions weaken and disappear[121]

Three types of pressures, shown on the left side of the figure, can cause institutions to weaken and disappear. *Competitive pressures* cause the utility or legitimacy of an institution to be called into question."[122] Such pressures arise because the practice is having a detrimental effect on organizational performance or its member commitment and is therefore simply being abandoned despite still being codified.[123] *Functional pressures* arise when the

[119] Christine Oliver, "The Antecedents of Deinstitutionalization," *Organization Studies* 13, no. 4 (1992): 563-588, 567.
[120] Scott, *Institutions and Organizations*, 171.
[121] Adapted from Oliver, "Antecedents," 567.
[122] Ibid., 568.
[123] Ibid., 567. Oliver's original term was "Political Pressure," however in practice all three categories of pressure achieve political effects on an organization or society. This was

increase in technical or administrative requirements exceeds the value of the institutional practice. As the practice becomes too complex or cumbersome, members may abandon it. Finally, *social pressures* can cause members to become fragmented over the value or utility of a practice, "causing divergent or discordant" beliefs.[124]

As political, functional, and social pressures cause an institution to weaken, two other types of pressures may present themselves, some trying (perhaps desperately) to preserve the presence while others hasten its dissolution. *Inertial pressures* constitutes an "active intervention to maintain the institution."[125] Oliver included the following are possible sources of inertia: (1) Investments in fixed assets that the institution relies on, which makes abandoning the practice costly; (2) Internal coordination that the practice facilitates, such that abandoning the practice would leave an uncomfortable void; (3) desires for predictability; (4) desires to show steadfastness and purpose; and (5) fear of disruption or stepping into the unknown.[126]

Accelerating the institution's demise are *entropic pressures*. Entropy is "a tendency toward disorganization in the social system"[127] that causes "erosion or decay in an institutional phenomenon."[128] In other words, left alone, any habit (except the most vital ones)[129] will eventual wither away and cease on their own because the organizational members will forget why the practice is in use, forget how to exercise the practice, or fail to transfer knowledge of the practice to new members.

An implication of this model is that breaking bad habits is difficult by leader dictum alone. The leader must choose which pressures to apply and what message to communicate to convince members to abandon the habit. This can mean presenting a clear

---

certainly true regarding social pressures leading to DADT's repeal. Oliver herself used "competitive pressure" synonymously.

[124] Scott, *Institutions and Organizations*, 169.

[125] Zucker, *Institutional Patterns*, 26.

[126] Oliver, "Antecedents," 580.

[127] Lynne G. Zucker, *Institutional Patterns and Organizations: Culture and Environment* (Cambridge, MA: Ballinger, 1988), 26.

[128] Oliver, "Antecedents," 580.

[129] Ibid.

and attractive alternative or sanctioning activities that protect the old way.

IMPLICATIONS FOR COMMUNICATION CAMPAIGNS

The complexity of large organizations mean it is likely that communication practices are imperfect in some way. The question for leaders is to what degree does the practice of communication foster or inhibit overall mission accomplishment. If communication is a problem, this chapter provides questions that leaders can ask to determine why. Is it that formal channels are failing to disseminate the messages across the organization as quickly or effectively as desired? Are rumors and misperceptions present and persistent such that the leader's messages are overwhelmed? Are there bad habits to break, such as activities that contribute to *say-do* gaps in the organization? Or, are there questions about *trust* or other indications of ineffective leader-member communication?

The lack of trust is often cited as a communication problem, but leaders should view it instead as something else. *Trust is an institutional practice*, which reflects the perceived legitimacy of formal authority and shared understandings about the levels of commitment that leaders demonstrate toward members and vice versa. Trust is also continuously subjected to entropic pressures — unless sustained by leaders and members alike, trust will dissipate. So when leaders hear that trust is a problem, what members are conveying is a symptom of the real problem, and the models in this chapter provides leaders with questions to help pursue the root causes. What occurred that created distrust? Was it a single communication or a sequence of communications that showed a lack of leader commitment to the members? Was it member recognition of say-do gaps by the organization? Was it the adoption of ill-advised or immature 'best practices' that created organizational inefficiency? Has the fall-out of a crisis damaged internal relationships?

Leaders should also investigate when its former good habits have perished and are no longer in practice. If members complain that the organization used to do something well but no longer, leaders can ask what pressures caused the organization to stop doing it. Was it internal or external? Personality-driven? Brought about by changes in the environment, legal restrictions, over-reaction to crises? Can the practice be restored or reset, as it was or in a modified form?

Another implication is that importance of treating the organizational membership as an audience, one whose employment of counternarratives against the organization can be quite effective. Leaders must understand how counternarratives enter the organization and spread among members. How and why do they persist despite leader communications promoting the organization's narrative?

The most important implication is the state of the relationship between leaders and members. If that relationship is unhealthy, it is very difficult for leaders to instill the desired communication posture and for desired leader messages to be received and accepted. As the next chapter will show, leaders of large organizations face an uphill battle in sustaining constructive internal and external relationships simultaneously.

CHAPTER 6. THE SENIOR LEADER'S STANDING CAMPAIGN

In Chapter 1, I presented the four communication roles of leaders. All leaders in the organization share responsibility for the execution of this roles, but the most senior leader — whether commander, director, secretary, or other title — has the ultimate authority and responsibility to see these roles through. The senior leader cannot delegate these responsibilities.

Senior leaders are vital to their success of their organizations' standing campaigns, regardless of whether they play active figurehead roles or operate in the background, generally hidden from public view. Senior leaders are the ultimate arbiters, developers, and communicators of the organizational narrative. Their abilities to convey narratives through personal words and deeds impact internal and external commitment to those narratives. Leaders failing to externalize narratives or creating say-do gaps in their personal examples will not see their campaigns succeed.

Many books and resources address the communication skills of leaders, such as how leaders prepare and deliver speeches, make appearances, and conduct engagements with the media. These are important, of course, but only at the tactical level of communication. What about the senior leader's effectiveness as a *campaigner?* What about developing and promulgating a successful personal-professional narrative, fending off attacks from others, establishing a rapport with others, and ensuring the smooth flow of information among oneself, one's personal staff, and the organization?

In other words, the senior leader (by virtue of being the senior leader) exercises a *personal standing campaign*[130] that comprises a melding of the senior leader's individual identity and interests with that of the organization's standing campaign. This personal campaign encompasses the integration of one's leadership style

---

[130] The use of 'personal' in this Primer is limited to one's professional persona or working identity (e.g., Herminia Ibarra). The natural extension of the idea to one's non-professional spheres such as family are beyond scope for present purposes.

and preferences with the organization's habits and practices, and helps the leader navigate the added criticism and negativity associated with being the senior leader of the organization.

WHAT IS THE LEADER'S *STANDING NARRATIVE*?

Looking at each assignment as an *episode* in one's career, individuals subsume components of the identities to each organization they belong.[131] Military officers experience significant periods of transition throughout their careers, involving major changes in duties, specializations, or duty locations. Previous transitions shape the leaders' approach to assumptions of senior leadership positions later.[132] Although the previous stated roles of leaders demand sacrificing individual identity in favor of the organizational identity, this is never done completely.[133] Rather, the assumption of leadership in the organization is an intervention at the personal level, and the leader's own identity changes as a result.[134] The same thing will occur when the leader departs, potentially to take on a different leadership position in a different organization. The leader will shed some aspects of the losing organization's identity and acquire aspects of the gaining. The sequence of actions fosters individual growth and change as the leader derives meaning from each episode, particularly those that are transformational and cause the leader to redefine "who am I?"[135]

The resulting story includes what is known as an *educational biography*, which captures "learning about one's own learning" rather than an autobiographical sequence of life events.[136] This

---

[131] Dennis A. Gioia, "From Individual to Organizational Identity," in David A. Whetten & Paul C. Godfrey (Eds.), *Identity in Organizations: Building Theory Through Conversations* (Thousand Oaks, CA: Sage, 1998).

[132] Thomas P. Galvin, *A Phenomenological Study of Identity Construction among Military Officers Promoted from the Middle Ranks to the Roles of Senior Leaders*, Doctoral Dissertation (Washington, DC: The George Washington University, 2015).

[133] Peter J. Burke, "Relationships among Multiple Identities," in Peter J. Burke, Timothy J. Owens, Richard T. Serpe, and Peggy A. Thoits (Eds.), *Advances in Identity Theory and Research* (New York: Kluwer, 2003).

[134] Herminia Ibarra, *Working Identity* (Cambridge, MA: Harvard Business Review Press, 2004).

[135] Thomas P. Galvin, *Enhancing Identity Development in Senior Service Colleges* (Carlisle, PA: U.S. Army War College Press, December 2016).

[136] Pierre Dominicé, *Learning from Our Lives: Using Educational Biographies with Adults* (San Francisco: Jossey-Bass, 2000), 1-5.

constitutes what I call the *leader's standing narrative*, as it captures how the leader will most likely use words and deeds while assuming and performing duties of senior leadership in an organization.

ARE COUNTERNARRATIVES DIRECTED AT LEADERS?

Yes, absolutely. Being a leader invariably means being criticized by someone. Counternarratives from outside the organization often use the leader as a proxy target to criticize the organization. It is immaterial whether or not the leader deserves it, as counternarratives serve the purposes of the opponent. Leaders are also prone to internal counternarratives that target the leader's standing narrative. Once a military assigns a leader to a command or executive billet, members of that organization are prone to gather information to learn likes, dislikes, preferences, idiosyncracies, etc. Those with negative experiences may share them with other members as a warning,[137] and will continue to accumulate during the leader's tenure.

The admonition about counternarratives from chapter 3 is therefore more than doubly true for the leader:

> *Everything leaders say, do, or are can and will be used against them.*
> *Everything leaders say not, do not, or are not, also can and will be used against them.*
> *AND*
> *Everything an organization says, does, or is can and will be used against the leaders.*
> *Everything an organization says not, does not, or is not, also can and will be used against the leaders.*
> *AND*
> *Everything that differs (real or perceived) among words, deeds, or identity between the organization and the leaders can and will be used against the leaders.*

Thus, the 6:1 asymmetric advantage of the opponent against the organization becomes effectively 15:1 against the leader.

---

[137] The process of 'G-2ing' was prevalent among the high-level organizations I served, particularly when the leader previously served as a staff director of the same command. The bad news stories, which were often exaggerated, spread fastest.

Certainly one expects that organizations and their leaders cannot avoid criticism, but for large complex organizations there is the important twist that some adversaries exist for the sole purposes of opposing the organization and its leaders--continuously shifting targets as older criticisms lose their salience with audiences.[138] Fortunately, there is an analyzable pattern against leaders that counternarratives take, similar to the types of counternarratives explained in Chapter 3.

Figure 7 shows a spectrum of counternarratives aimed at persons in leadership positions. This spectrum reflects differences in tone from the rational to the emotional. On the rational side, counternarratives redress demonstrable shortcomings and seek corrective action. Some such counternarratives may be friendly. On the opposite end, counternarratives use emotionally-constructed alternative persona of target leaders to divert attention away from the leaders' true words or actions, and instead portray the leaders as evil, reckless, or dangerously incompetent. In effect, the counternarrative reduces the leader to a symbol for hatred in hopes of isolating them from the organization, stakeholders, or the environment. On the rational side, purveyors of the counternarratives are more likely to welcome engagement with the leader. Purveyors of emotional counternarratives are more likely to either avoid direct contact or, if contact occurs, to misrepresent any discussions that took place.

Leader Must Go counternarratives are the most rational, emerging as the result of: (a) the organization has failed and therefore the leader has failed, or (b) the leader has done something unacceptable (or reprehensible) and therefore the organization no longer has faith or confidence in the leader. If the organization does not act against the leader, member commitment to the organization is at risk.

---

[138] Galvin, *Two Case Studies*, includes a discussion of such entities in the USAFRICOM case, where organizations formed specifically to force policymakers to cease the command's creation. Because of unfounded fears over USAFRICOM, their messages spread widely. But when it became apparent that the command was moving forward, new counternarratives appeared that targeted the commander as a puppet of the imperialist U.S. agenda. When that failed, they shifted back to the organization; this time attacking the command's activities. When that failed, they began new attacks against the commander by pulling words out of context and claiming he was being duplicitous. It took a few years before the opponents no longer had grounds to criticize the command or its leader.

	'Leader Must Go'		'Coaching Change'		'Detached Leadership'	'Leader is Evil'
Aim	Corrective	– –	Pre-emptive	– –	Isolating the Collective Leadership	Isolating the Individual Leader
Character	Leader culpable	· – –	Leader is scapegoat	– – –	Leader dismissive/ ambivalent	Polemic, crude, dehumanizing
Causation	Linked to an identifiable cause	· – – ·	Did not address problems adequately	· – – – – ·	Did not care enough	– – ·	Causation not required
Engagement	Engaging leader necessary to legitimize criticism	– ·	Engaging leader helps but is not necessary	– –	Engaging leader is assumed to be fruitless	– ·	Avoids engaging leader at all costs

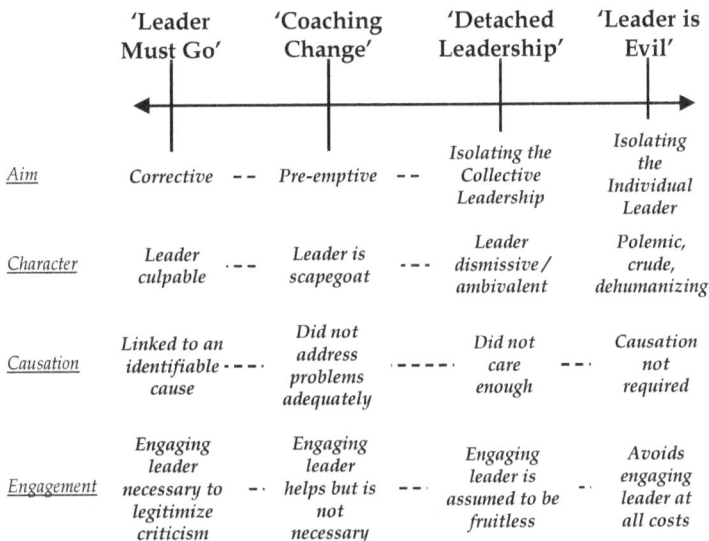

Figure 7. Spectrum of Anti-Leader Counternarratives[139]

Objective (tangible) factors can make such counternarratives powerful. The visible failure of the organization in accomplishing a mission or clear legal, ethical, or moral violations of the leader provide compelling evidence of an insurmountable problem, even when the leader provides a suitable and justifiable explanation. Messages from such counternarratives usually emphasize the direct culpability of the leader, warn of assured repeat of the offenses or failures, and call into question other leader or organizational accomplishments.

Further down the spectrum are counternarratives emerging when the organization fails and the leader is targeted more by circumstances. Drawing from a sports metaphor, _coaching change_ counternarratives emerge either from unmet expectations or a need to reverse a downward trend to pre-empt failure. However, the problems and concerns may not be perceived as bad enough to warrant wider organizational transformation. Thus, like in professional sports, when the players are playing badly, firing the

---

[139] Original graphic by author based on Galvin, _Two Case Studies_, especially the USAFRICOM case.

coach is often more expedient and seemingly sufficient than trading away underperforming star players.

There are several variants to this type of counternarrative that leaders face: (a) when members desire to wait until a leader departs rather than confront the leader directly, (b) accusing the leader of change for change sake or otherwise rebelling against a leader initiative, (c) comparing the leader unfavorably to a predecessor or other alternative leader, (d) if the leader does not fit the ingroup prototype, view the leader as some sort of outsider, (e) question the leader's motivation for leader (e.g., punching tickets or riding coattails), or (f) assuming that the leader is a stakeholder's puppet or blindly following an external mandate.

The third type, *detached leadership* counternarratives reify an abstract 'leadership' entity and criticize it in lieu of criticizing any individual leader by name. This is only partly rational in that the purveyors of such counternarratives are less interested in getting to the bottom of a problem and instead pass the blame to an untraceable other. 'Leadership,' 'head shed,' 'front office,' 'brass,' 'puzzle palace,' and the 'Pentagon'[140] are thus responsible for any word or deed that members find opaque, inconsistent, counterproductive, or mystifying. Messages from these counternarrative often take on qualities of urban legends, conspiracy theories, or hidden agendas transcending any individual leader. Odd or inexplicable leader actions are claimed to result from a pernicious leadership culture or immutable organizational environment.

Variants of these counternarratives include:

- *'The Leadership Does Not Listen'* – Stems from angst concerning the perceived lack of control or input that members or stakeholders have in organizational decisions. Messages emerging from this counternarrative might: (1)

---

[140] This is an example of a *metonym*, which is "a figure of speech consisting of the use of the name of one thing for that of another of which it is an attribute or with which it is associated," from Merriam-Webster, s.v. "metonym," https://www.merriam-webster.com/dictionary/metonymy (accessed 18 January 2017). Some military organizations use building names or numbers, or named/numbered parts of buildings such as a 'wing' or 'floor' within a building as a metonym for the organization's leadership. For example, members of the U.S. Army War College may reference the 'A Wing,' the part of the main building's 1st floor where the College's command group offices reside.

dismiss or question attempts by leaders to engage the stakeholder, (2) lament perceived lack of tangible evidence that leaders act on stakeholder suggestions or recommendations, or (3) dislike or distrust the organization and use specific examples of organizational decisions to justify their negative stance.

- *'The Leadership Does Not Care'* – Regards angst over perceived imbalances between concerns for mission accomplishment and the health, morale, and welfare of its people. This may surface when organizations are fighting for survival or otherwise under pressure and the mission becomes more salient at the members' expense. External actors empathize the disadvantaged position of the members and attribute it to the leaders. It also can stem from member or stakeholder reactions to leader communication (including body language or decision making) regarding its people.

- *'The Leadership Already Made Up Its Mind'* – a variant of 'Does Not Listen,' this counternarrative is active when a change is pursued without any apparent member or stakeholder input. Socializing the change effort is seen with skepticism as a vain effort to justify a *fait accompli*.[141]

The extremely emotional counternarratives characterize the leader as *Evil*. This is a loaded choice of words because the word evil carries many connotations. As applied here, the senior leader is incapable of doing good such that there is no purpose for treating them well. These counternarratives are little more than well-constructed *ad hominem* ('against the person') attacks that show little empathy toward their targets. In effect, the counternarratives assume that opposing leaders must be vilified just for being opposing leaders. After all the leader is the figurehead of the organization and therefore any sins of the organization also supposedly belong to the leader. Those who use

---

[141] Draws from the USAFRICOM Case Study (Galvin, *Two Case Studies*, Chapter 3) and the perceptions of Department of State members that the Department of Defense entered into interagency negotiations already having made up its mind, and had the resources to exercise its will over interagency decisions. The State officials used the term *fait accompli* to describe Defense's imposition and unwillingness to negotiate.

such counternarratives do not wish direct engagement with the leader because that legitimizes the leader, which is not what the opponent wants. Moreover, the opponent fears being viewed as soft on the leader by like-minded others. The counternarrative makes no room for mercy.

Do leaders use counternarratives?

Senior leaders can (and do) use these same counternarratives against leaders of other organizations, with two key differences. First, as leaders of professional military organizations, senior leaders do not have the same freedom to fabricate messages against opponents. Certainly, they can characterize deserving opponents as "evil" (e.g., against leaders of violent extremist organizations). However, they must be able to justify such words through evidence lest their own professional identities be called into question. Although it may seem like an unfair advantage the opponents have, lying in the modern environment is risky. Opponents who lie outright often overlook the consequences of being exposed as liars, an increasingly likely prospect given today's information technologies. One significant risk is the opponent isolating itself as media and others refuse to grant the opponent an audience. In contrast, sustaining professional integrity allows senior leaders greater access to media to present their messages.

The second key difference is the requirement to synchronize one's own communications with national policy. That is, one cannot speak or act toward opponent without due consideration of the potential impacts on other government activities. Mixed messages between military and civilian agencies, no matter how justified each agency leader may be, presents a potential problem for national leaders. In this way, opponents appear to have an advantage in being able to generate messages with less regard to consequences over their partners, while senior leaders put themselves at professional risk when they speak or act differently than what is expected or approved by national leaders. On the other hand, senior leaders recognize more directly how the military is but one subordinate organization in the national government—and the government's standing campaign (which in the U.S. includes civilian control over the military) normally takes precedence.

Of course, the professional identity of the military requires that leaders speak up when national policy is wrong in some way. When national security and the readiness of the military are at unacceptable risk, these are threats to the military's standing campaign and the senior leader has an obligation to address them. The question becomes a matter of when, where, and how, especially the situation requires deviation from the practices of communication at the national level.

HOW DO LEADERS DEFEND THEMSELVES FROM ATTACK?

That leaders must respond to criticism throughout their tenures is hardly news, and perceptions of leader efficacy is often enhanced by leaders who handle criticism well and constructively.[142] The modeling of leader counternarratives above suggests that criticism does not act as a series of discrete words or actions but as sustained patterns of alternative (often negative) message generation. When rational, this pattern appears as routine scrutinizing of the leader's actions – everything the leaders says or does is subject to critique. When emotional, the pattern appears as continuous streams of hostility – everything the leader is or is assumed to be becomes a persistent source of invective. In either case, leaders will find that responding to individual statements fails to have sufficient impact. The criticisms will evolve to confront or avoid the response, and the underlying counternarrative will be little affected.

There are several types of defensive narratives that leaders can choose to defend themselves and their organizations. Four are explained here. First is an *authenticity* defense. Authenticity is a desirable characteristic of leader communication in general,[143] but it can also be invoked as a defense against emotional attacks through a story combining 'the attack is not true' with 'I would not have said that.' This deflects the attack and provides room to

---

[142] Ibid., 365.
[143] Herminia Ibarra, "The Authenticity Paradox," *Harvard Business Review*, Vol. 93, No. 1/2 (Jan-Feb 2015): 53-59.

explain the leader's preferred message and demonstrate that the message belongs to the leader and no one else.

A second defensive narrative uses *different frames of reference*. This is also a deflective approach. The purpose is to isolate the counternarrative by demonstrating how it takes the 'wrong' perspective of something. Taking the 'right' view negates the opponent's claims. The change of perspective takes some character of the opponent's message and reverses it. For example, if the leader perceives that counternarratives are overly focused at the details of something, the leader may develop C-CNs that tell a more abstract story and generate messages that paint the forest rather than the trees.

A third defense is to *channel the opponent's targeting*. In other words, reduce the opponent's advantage from 15-to-1 to something much smaller by making certain forms of counternarrative seem attractive. For example, the leader may decide to become a lightning rod and personally absorb criticism to allow other parts of the organization to take action.

A similar form is the *red line* defense, which is most applicable in cases where one's primary stakeholder is an opponent, and the organization is having to protect itself in some way from possibly undesirable stakeholder decisions. The leader essentially uses a defensive strategy of mitigation to maintain a constructive relationship with the stakeholder unless certain conditions hold, in which the leader switches to a more confrontational approach.

When must leaders personally deliver messages?

The answer to this question is often established in the leaders' personal standing campaigns. Their identities and personalities suggest how much they prefer to stand in or eschew the spotlight. It also expresses the leader's preferences on how communication occurs — such as told through words or shown through personal example. If their preferences align with the organization's preferences in its standing campaign, there is less need for the leader to adapt to the organizational environment. But as stewards of the organization's narrative and embodiment of the organization, situations can pressure leaders to be more public than they would prefer, or require leaders to make difficult choices over which messages they must deliver. Often, these occur from external pressures – such as a stakeholder demand or crisis situation – and the leader's options are limited.

The more important and difficult decisions regard in less extraordinarily circumstances when the leader has the full range of options available from total engagement to total delegation, but defaults to following one's personal preference. This may lead to confusion within the organization if members are in need of the leader's personal communication to: (1) reassure the membership, (2) clarify contradictory stories or information, or (3) relay a vision or overall strategic direction. Based on my experiences, below are four situations where the leader must step forward and be the lead communicator on behalf of the organization.

First is when the leader initiates the use of counternarratives against a stakeholder or other friendly or allied audience. As stated earlier in this book, organizations do use counternarratives against their friends (and vice versa). Usually, it is a matter of disagreement or different perspectives yet unresolved. But to have such disagreements surface second-hand without direct leader legitimization is dangerous and can create unnecessary tension. The leader must legitimize the dispute through personal messaging, which in turn provides the parameters and guidance to allow members to act on the dispute with confidence.

Second, and most commonly, is a matter of protocol. Certain audiences will feel slighted or insulted by what they feel is second-hand engagement with organizational members rather than the leader. Another circumstance is when the leader engages with a lower-tiered entity first.[144] These cases are often easily identified, but it may be difficult to follow strict protocol due to scheduling and other conflicts. In such cases, the burden falls upon the leader to exercise additional messaging to explain the situation and ensure no harm is done.

The third situation is when *ambivalence* and *complacency* are deemed to be high, and the leader must set the stage for change. In essence, audiences (members or stakeholders) need a swift

---

[144] An example of this being avoided was in the early days of USAFRICOM when the commander delayed or deferred all country-level engagements until he had a chance to visit the African Union. See Galvin, *Two Case Studies*.

kick. Although later chapters will show that much messaging in named campaigns is delegated naturally, the initial shock to the system is best delivered by the senior leader.

Fourth is crisis. When the organization is under intense pressure, regardless of what caused the crisis, the leader has a mandatory responsibility to absorb the added attention and provide the organizational members with freedom to maneuver – ostensibly to correct the crisis situation. Leader communications under such circumstances serves to: (1) reassure, (2) clarify the situation, and (3) set direction. These should guide the organization toward unified action despite the intense pace and conflicting information regarding the crisis situation.

IMPLICATIONS FOR LEADERS

So much of what occurs in communication campaigns involves the leader personally or is a reflection of the leader's wishes. In the standing campaign, the leader is a natural target in the ordinary competitive environment. Opponents of the organization will associate every flaw of that organization on the leader and vice versa. Named campaigns, as leader interventions, mean that leaders are placing their reputations on the line. Meanwhile, the lack of named campaigns can also trigger criticism, such as the leader being complacent or behind the times. Under the 15-to-1 advantage of the critics, the leader cannot avoid criticism. One might therefore assume that service as a leader under these conditions can be difficult for the thin-skinned. In reality, however, having a thick skin can be a liability if it means the leader is de-sensitized toward the needs of the organization's members or external stakeholders.[145]

Leaders face difficult choices when it comes to communicating to change the organization. They will likely not be able to personally champion every campaign they wish at the desired intensity; there is neither enough time nor personal energy. Thus the role of governing the communication process is very important. If leaders succeed at demonstrating what right

---

[145] Lucy Kellaway, "Why Good Leaders Should Dump the Thick-Skinned Approach," *Globe and Mail*, June 19, 2012, https://www.theglobeandmail.com/report-on-business/careers/careers-leadership/why-good-leaders-should-dump-the-thick-skinned-approach/article4327380/ (accessed 19 April 2018).

looks like in a few campaigns, they hope and expect that the members will follow suit and initiate additional campaigns on their own. Calls for 'cultures of innovation,' for example, seek to do just that.

Leaders of large military organizations face a particularly difficult challenge because external demands can preclude the leader from being active within the organization on a day-to-day basis. This role is thus often delegated to a second-in-command or a chief of staff. While the division of labor is logical, it is also risky if leaders become so consumed with the external environment that they become strangers to their own organizations. This may be OK when the organization is performing well and members are satisfied and committed, but might not be OK when the organization is facing difficulties.

A second implication is that leaders need not be on the defensive. Each counternarrative is available for the leader's use against opposing leaders. In other words, leaders need not just take punches, they can dish them out, too! However, leaders in professional organizations must be mindful of the impact that attacking other leaders has on the reputation of the organization. After all, leaders who attack others will invite attacks on themselves, and potentially drag the organization's members into the fray. Inviting attack can prove to be a distraction or irritant to the organization's stakeholders.

Hence, leaders should avoid using 'personal' counternarratives and lean toward the more reasoned or objective side of the spectrum shown in **Error! Reference source not found.**. For example, rational errors by the opponent should be responded to with rational criticism, such as claims that the opponent is incompetent. Even if the opponent is irrational or dangerous and evil, criticizing in kind without a rational argument to underpin could cause audiences to view the leader as hysterical or paranoid. A more objective critique, such as a 'coaching change' counternarrative, allows the leader to maintain a professional reputation and stake the moral high ground.

The third implication is that the leader should also carefully choose a personal defensive strategy that protects *both* self and the organization. Defensive narratives that appear to protect the self at the organization's expense will backfire quickly, and the leader's reputation can be destroyed. However, the leader's personal defense should endure beyond one's tenure in the organization. This is because everything that the leader 'does, says, or is' endures two ways – establishing the legacy in the organization and following the leader to future assignments in other organizations. A personal strategy that is too context-driven risks being inconsistently applied.

Three elements of a personal defensive strategy are suggested here. First is how the leader maintains *authenticity*. Authenticity is an important characteristic of leader communication.[146] The leader's personality ultimately determines the best ordinary defensive strategy. Leaders cannot and should not respond outside of their personality as a matter of course. If they are rational thinkers and speakers, they should respond to criticisms rationally. If they are emotive, then they should communicate with emotion. Defensive messages will be more successful if perceived as authentically coming from the leader and not someone else.

The second regards how to deal with opponents who are also stakeholders. If the primary stakeholder is an adversarial entity or is readily influenced by adversarial messages, the organization will often be on the defense trying to protect itself from disadvantageous decisions, such as reductions in resources. In such circumstances, the leader's personal reputation sets the tone for the defensive strategy. If known as a fighter, the leader should defend by confronting the stakeholders. If known as a collaborator, the leader should defend through aggressive engagement. In either case, the underlying messaging must still come from the organization's narrative and not the leader, otherwise the leader will appear to taking matters too personally.

Third, the strategy should question to what degree the leader sacrifices self for the good of the organization. Military culture prefers that the captain go down with ship, but this does not make for a good communication strategy as it encourages opponents to be aggressive and force the leaders into no-win situations. In

---

[146] Herminia Ibarra, "The Authenticity Paradox," *Harvard Business Review*, Vol. 93, No. 1/2 (Jan-Feb 2015): 53-59.

reality, many communication campaigns involve negotiation in which the leader may have to put elements of the organizational narrative on the table. Leaders have to understand where the line is that the negotiation must not cross — those aspects of the narrative that must be defended at all costs. It is therefore important for leaders to be self-aware about how they draw such lines and communicate them to organizational members.

Finally, what happens to campaigns that the leader does not personally champion? Campaigns can succeed with little or no leader direct involvement, however the scope of the campaign may be reduced to that of the subordinate leader who is delegated as new champion. For example, a campaign delegated to a chief of staff becomes a headquarters staff campaign, with the leader becoming a primary stakeholder and the subordinate organizations becoming external audiences. The chief of staff competes for the leader's attention and priority, and negotiates the roles that suborganizations play. So long as the leader sustains a constructive stakeholder relationship and stays engaged, even if occasionally, the organization can still pursue the campaign.

CHAPTER 7. HOW TO INITIATE A NAMED CAMPAIGN?

It is one thing to have a standing campaign with messages, audiences, and processes, but what does one *do* with it? More directly, when should a leader intervene and establish a named campaign? Before answering that question, it is helpful to understand the various functions that both standing and named campaigns perform. These are shown in Figure 8.

- *Promote the Narrative* – Campaigns demonstrate through words and actions that the organization's narrative is truthful and relevant. They provide ways and means for the organizational members to further promote the narrative with minimal leader intervention. In essence, campaigns help narratives sell themselves.

- *Defend the Narrative* – Others use *counternarratives* to attack the organization's narrative. Thus, organizations must defend their narrative by denying and discrediting the opposing view, or countering with alternative perspectives.

- *Target others' Narratives* – Organizations also go on the offense, crafting and deploying counternarratives to either attack their adversaries' narratives, or present alternative perspectives to the narratives of partners and stakeholders.

- *Adapt the Narrative* – The narrative, like the identity, is stable but not static. To keep its competitive advantage, organizations must adapt their narrative, sometimes to accommodate the legitimate criticisms of partners and stakeholders.

Put simply, leaders intervene with a named campaign when the standing campaign is insufficient or deficient in some way. As stewards of the narrative, leaders have an obligation to intervene and correct messaging problems. As governors of the process, leaders must address communication problems preventing the proper dissemination of the right information and countering misinformation and disinformation as close to the sources as possible. But named campaigns are complex and require much effort to develop and synchronize. The next section summarizes the process for initiating and implementing a named campaign.

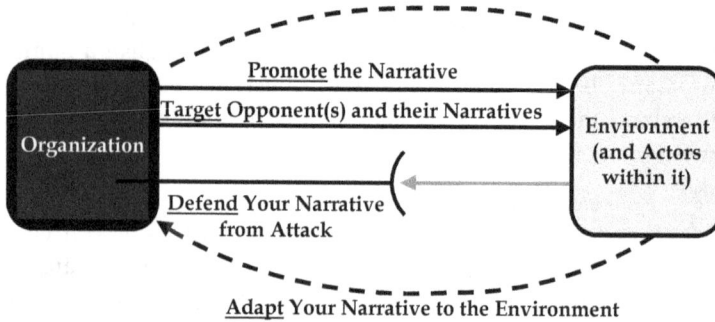

Figure 8. Four Functions of a Named Campaign[147]

Campaigning begins when the leader communicates the need for a campaign to another individual. This implies that many campaigns end after a single conversation, but that conversation produces an understanding of leader intent which in turn sends a signal to the organization. As knowledge of the campaign widens, long before it is launched, members and stakeholders alike may choose to join or resist it. Rumors and stories about the campaign, which may or may not be true, may spread. Thus the period between inception of the idea and the launch of the campaign, a period of *pre-launch*, is very important. Leaders must use the pre-launch period to both properly socialize and structure the campaign.

Hence, it is recommended that the leader conduct an analysis and begin formulation of the campaign internally and engage with others thereafter. If the proverbial 'cat' is out of the 'bag' too soon, the leader may forfeit the initiative and be unable to guide the organization's response to the leader's ideas in a productive fashion. In effect, this chapter provides a methodology for the leader to develop a personal campaign for initiating an organizational communication campaign. It is less important that this personal campaign be complete, but that the leader has sufficiently reflected on the current state of the organization to

---

[147] Original graphic by author.

engage with internal and external audiences from a position of strength and knowledge. It will reduce leader defensiveness toward the organization's reactions and resistance, encourage empathy and participative decision making, help the leader evolve the purpose and content of the budding campaign, and ultimately foster better feasibility, suitability, and acceptance of the campaign prior to launch.

Figure 9 shows the roadmap. The remainder of this chapter covers the first two bubbles on the right hand side—setting purpose and vision and developing themes and messages. The leader in solitude develops ideas for these which are carried into the pre-launch discussions and negotiated. The two bubbles in the later chapters are pursed as the leader determines that indeed the campaign will launch.

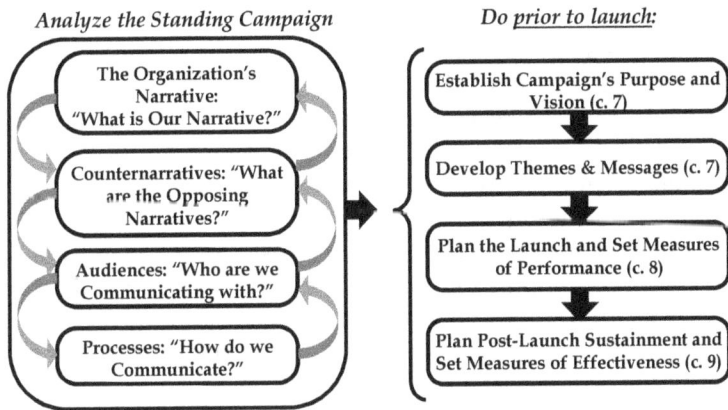

Analyze the Standing Campaign   *Do <u>prior to launch</u>:*

The Organization's Narrative: "What is Our Narrative?"

Counternarratives: "What are the Opposing Narratives?"

Audiences: "Who are we Communicating with?"

Processes: "How do we Communicate?"

Establish Campaign's Purpose and Vision (c. 7)

Develop Themes & Messages (c. 7)

Plan the Launch and Set Measures of Performance (c. 8)

Plan Post-Launch Sustainment and Set Measures of Effectiveness (c. 9)

Figure 9. Pre-Launch Requirements of a Campaign[148]

A final note on pre-launch is that at any time, the leader can stop the campaign with relatively little difficulty. However once launched, a campaign is difficult to stop without causing harm to the organization's narrative. The more deliberate thought and planning that goes into pre-launch, the better chance of success the campaign will have.

---

[148] Original graphic by author.

Five Steps to Initiating Named Campaigns?

Named campaign initiation is a five-step process that begins when the leader determines the current content and practices of communication are deficient, such that either or both must change. As implied in Chapter 1, named campaigns are forms of organizational change, and may at times accompany structural change in the organization. Certainly, any transformational change will have a communication component to explain to members and external audiences what is changing and why, and how it may or may not affect them. But a communication campaign may stand alone, such as when misperceptions or confusion abound. Such campaigns may serve to reinforce the standing narrative, correct misperceptions, and reassure members — effectively changing minds, not structures or processes necessarily.

The five steps are depicted in Figure 10. The first two steps are diagnostic and allow the leader to determine whether or not a new named campaign is necessary, or that perhaps an existing campaign can be leveraged. First, the planner reviews the specific stimulus or impetus from the environment and analyzes it to determine how it influences the organization. Is it a type of crisis, and if so what form? Or, is it a lack of crisis leading to the onset of complacency or other cultural issues that cause the organization to deviate from its narrative? The second step establishes the purpose for the campaign. What is the desired future state of the organization such that the narrative is self-promoting and the organization is better postured to defend itself and attack opponents? Steps 3 through 5 construct the architecture of the campaign – the campaign vision, concept, and key themes and messages.

Step 1. Describe the Impetus for the Campaign

The goal of this activity is to identify the senior leader's personal perspective, preferences, and environment. The level of detail required will depend on the campaign. The stimulus of the campaign carries with it the qualities of a crisis, disrupting the *status quo* of the organization. Otherwise, there would be no need for the campaign. Crisis scholar Steve Gundel developed a typology of four types of crises which organizations face. The typology is built on two axes – the *predictability* of the crisis (easy or hard) and the *influenceability* over the crisis by the organization (easy or hard).

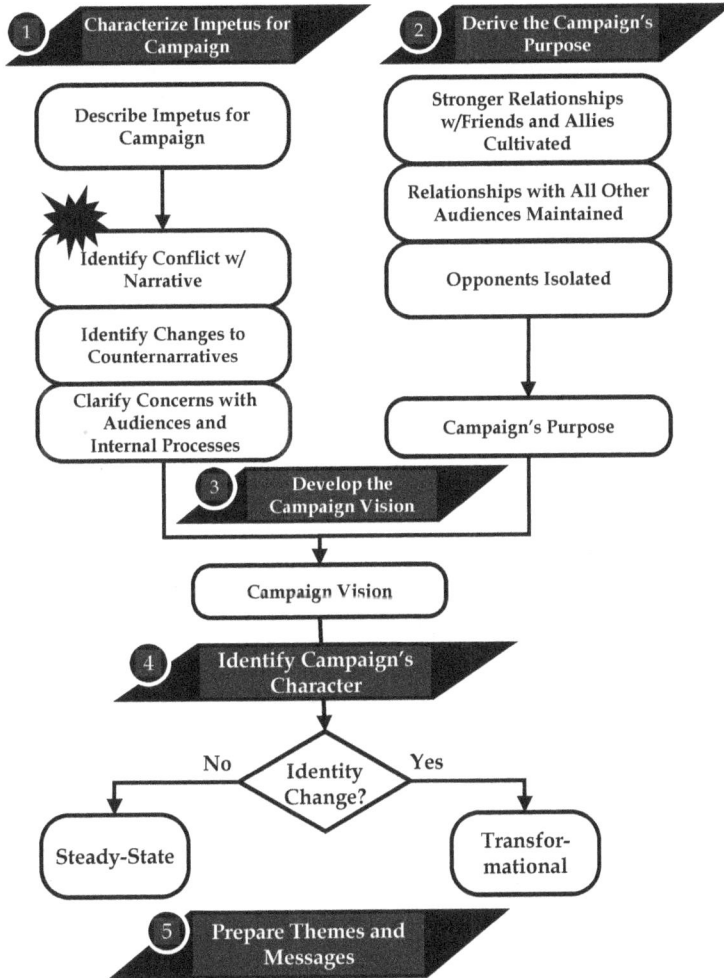

Figure 10. Five Steps for Pre-Launch[149]

- *Conventional* (easily predictable and influenceable). These sorts of crises are those that the organization would ordinarily be expected to handle without much leader

---

[149] Original graphic by author.

intervention. Snow removal in cold-weather cities is an example – failure to respond to a snow event would appear very problematic for the city.

- *Unexpected* (not predictable but easily influenceable). Unexpected crisis situations come about when the hazard is not foreseen or foreseeable, thereby inhibiting direct preventative measures. Yet, the organization still has the capability or capacity to respond, probably in novel or unforeseen ways. On the other hand, poor responses may cause the organization to appear flat-footed and not adaptive. In the snow removal case, an unpredictable event might be the introduction of an oversized load being transported over a highway during an unexpected snowfall. The subsequent crash and closure of the highways would be an unexpected crisis as snow removal and first responders would face a dangerous and complex situation.

- *Intractable* (predictable but not influenceable). Some crises are ones that can be foreseen but are beyond the organization's capability or capacity to prevent or respond to them. In essence, one can take prudent steps to prepare, but otherwise the organization is forced to react as the crisis unfolds. Natural disasters easily fall in this category. Earthquakes, volcanic eruptions, hurricanes, tornadoes, floods and the like are generally predictable in the sense that certain parts of the world have a propensity to experience certain types.

- *Fundamental* (neither predictable nor influenceable). These crises are the doomsday scenarios, where the hazard could not be foreseen and the organization is generally incapable of preventing or influencing the crisis. Ordinarily, these would be extremely rare and powerful. Natural examples would include the worst of all possible earthquakes and tsunamis. The catastrophic failure of the Internet or the Global Positioning System that so much of society depends is another example. These sorts of crises are those that the organization would ordinarily be expected to handle without much leader intervention. Snow removal in cold-weather cities is an example – failure to respond to a snow event would appear very problematic for the city.

The application of this crisis typology is straightforward for external stimuli, but less so for internal stimuli. The following rules of thumb may be helpful. An internal crisis is predictable if it constitutes some sort of violation of the organization's narrative. For example, a rule or regulation was broken, a norm was abandoned or ceased to function, or a shared understanding is clearly misaligned with reality. These are predictable because they constitute common organizational errors or missteps, deviations from what the organization should have done or is expected to have done. An internal crisis is also predictable if it draws from a recognized tension – either vertically up the hierarchy or horizontally across networks. If it is known that lower echelons distrust the leadership or that silos or rivalries inhibit collaboration, then crises along those lines are predictable. That they may not have been necessarily foreseen does not mean they are not predictable.

In contrast, an internal crisis may be not predictable if it is created from an unforeseen negative effect stemming from the normal or proper functioning of the organization. If following a rule creates a surprising second-order effect, then the crisis from it might not be predictable. An internal crisis may also be not predictable if it comes from a novel or unique schism in the organization that differs from other extant tensions.

An internal crisis is influenceable if the organization has the resources and capacity to address the crisis situation adequately. Inactivity due to inconvenience to the organization does not make the crisis less influenceable. An internal crisis is not influenceable if it is clearly and unequivocally beyond the organization's resources.

With the crisis understood, leaders should then put it in terms of the standing narrative. What is the conflict, or in what ways does the crisis threaten the narrative? Is the identity of the organization threatened in some way? Will the crisis diminish the organization's competitive advantage, or intensify its disadvantage? Leaders can also look at how opponents and competitors are using the crisis for their own gain, or to strengthen counternarratives against the organization.

Leader should also look at how the crisis is influencing external and internal audiences, particularly stakeholders. Are they shifting their opinions of the organization or changing their relationships with it? Are they withholding support on other areas, or taking a wait-and-see approach? Internal audiences may see the crisis as a means of unifying and strengthening resolve, or exacerbating existing divisions. Leaders should inquire how formal and informal channels are being used or bypassed, and what rumors, legends, and other stories are overtaking the organization's preferred messages.

From this analysis, the need for the named campaign should be apparent. Leaders should determine to what extent *not* exercising a named campaign would allow all these factors stemming the crisis to cause harm to the narrative. That becomes the impetus.

Step 2. Derive the Campaign's Purpose

The second activity connects the stimulus to the organization's image and reputation, thereby answering the question *what does a successful future for the organization look like after the campaign is complete*? The desired state is composed of the elements of a transformed or evolved organizational image and reputation from the perspectives of stakeholders and all other audiences. In what ways must relationships with stakeholders and friendly audiences be strengthened or sustained? What about fence-sitters, must some necessarily be converted to allies or is it sufficient that they not side with opponents? Of course, the desired future state must consider opponents. What does it mean for the opponents to be isolated, and their counternarratives also isolated?

There are two rules of thumb to consider when articulating this change, and they will sound contradictory. The first rule of thumb is that *less mandated change is better*. That is, the campaign may aspire to change the organization's reputation on many front, but its measures of success should be focused and not depend on the views of too many audiences. For example, steady-state campaigns sustain or restore the status quo against an impetus that threatens it. Hence, in many cases the goal is to prevent or limit change, particularly of stakeholders. Transformational campaigns will accompany a change effort and therefore structural change and norms within the organization will change, but that does not necessarily mean that the campaign's purpose is to change a lot of relationships. Instead, the campaign should focus on those relationships that absolutely must change for the campaign to succeed—such as particular stakeholders who are reticent to give needed resources to the effort, or a particularly unique counternarrative that threatens the transformative change. So, leader should ask questions such as the following: (1) what change is necessary to the accomplishment of the campaign's goals? (2) Which new opponents must be isolated? (3) What counternarratives are critical to address? (4) What must the new internal communication processes look like to address internal resistance to the change effort?

A second rule of thumb is that campaigns should *shoot for the stars*. The challenge for leaders is that the minimum purpose inspires minimum effort. A ways to reconcile the apparent contradiction with the first rule of thumb is that successful campaign should enable additional campaigns. This is about enhancing the organization's projected image, which may in turn not necessarily improve the organization's reputation but at least helps ensure the organization is better known or better liked. Aspirational goals could also spur independent actions by members that are aligned with the campaign and feed into future campaigns. In short, because the purpose of the named campaign is to promote and adapt the standing campaign, leaders should never look at a single named campaign in isolation of all other organizational activity.

Step 3. Write the Campaign Vision

The leader now has defined the current state and desired future state as a result of the communication campaign. It is now time to put the desired future state in practical and actionable terms as a delta of the current narrative. Like the narrative, the vision is more than the bumper sticker, it is a prose description of the impetus for change, the challenge it presents to the current narrative, the purpose of the campaign and, most importantly, why the campaign is the best solution to achieve the desired end state.

The story must be told in concrete terms as much as possible. This bears emphasis because a campaign vision that is too esoteric, abstract, or impractical cannot be communicated effectively across a wide array of audiences. The vision must both explain and justify the desired state, effectively making clear the highway or footpath leading to the future.

However, just because the leader has written a campaign vision does *not* mean it will be disseminated as is. The vision may contain sensitive information and not be releasable in total, or in the case of military organizations could be classified. For example, explicit naming of adversaries and identification of counternarratives can be inflammatory if known outside the organization, and premature knowledge of the campaign vision inside the organization could allow opponents to mobilize resistance. The choices of themes and messages in Step 5 becomes critical because the organization may have to pursue the campaign without ever being able to tell the entire story.

Step 4: Identify Campaign's Character

Is the campaign steady-state or transformational? This step may seem trivial and obvious, but it is not. Just because the organization is undergoing a transformational change does *not* mean that the communication campaign will be transformational! Moreover, steady-state activities may require a transformational communication campaign! It depends entirely on the degree to which the campaign changes the organization's narrative, which in turn drives the choices of themes and messages, measures of performance and effectiveness, and termination conditions.

Step 5. Identify Key Themes and Messages

The final step concentrates on the substance behind the narrative – the development of subordinate themes and messages that apply throughout the campaign. Narratives are too broad and complex to plan individual speeches and events around. Consequently, leaders need to divide the narrative into useful elements to help set communication priorities and synchronize activities. Themes and messages represent two levels of a hierarchy, bringing the narrative to progressively more concrete forms with clearer focus on specific audiences. Whereas narratives are persistent and portray a projected image of the organization, *themes* relate to central "topics" or "representations" pertaining to a specific communication or engagement.[150] For example, if the U.S. Army's narrative is about being a being a premier Landpower force, themes promoting that narrative might include the following:

- U.S. Army's historical success as a Landpower force, which foretells its continued pursuit of excellence into the future

- U.S. Army's current dominance in Landpower due to its powerful and versatile weapons systems platforms

- Professionalism of the U.S. Army Soldier

Leader input is critical, as developing themes and messages is an art. Given the campaign vision, how does a planner divide it into usable themes for delivery to broad audiences, and further divide the themes into tailorable messages for delivery? There is no prescribed way to divide a vision into component parts – it depends greatly on the organization and its leaders. Consider the following as three important rules of thumb. First, the sum of all themes should equal or exceed the campaign's vision. Second, the sum of all messages within a theme should equal or exceed the meaning of the theme. Finally, assume that opponents will misuse any message of the campaign so do not attempt to make bullet-proof messages. Such messages can be bland and uninspiring, or all things to all people, and will not serve the campaign well.

The two tables below include some general classes of themes as a start point for any campaign. Table 3 lists common themes for steady-state campaigns, while Table 4 adds common themes

---

[150] This is drawn from the definition of *theme* in literary studies – "a subject or topic of discourse or of artistic representation" from Merriam Webster, s.v. *Theme*, http://www.merriam-webster.com/dictionary/theme (retrieved 27 July 2015). *Discourse*, from http://www.merriam-webster.com/dictionary/discourse (retrieved 27 July 2015), refers more to verbal communication and not actions.

applicable for a transformational campaign, where the organizational identity does change.

Table 3. Common Themes for 'Steady-State' Campaigns (No Change to Identity)[151]

Themes of ...	Function(s)	Description	Desired Effects
Excellence	Promote	Celebrates identity Promotes competitive advantage (current and future)	Member commitment increased Stakeholders convinced of org.'s value
Stability	Defend	Discredits charges of complacency and risk aversion Presents organization's strengths, resilience, camaraderie, reliability	As above, plus... Counternarratives isolated and abandoned
Constantly Improving	Defend & Adapt	Emphasizes learning and innovation, embracing new ideas Discredits charges of complacency and risk aversion	As above, plus... Stakeholders support improvement efforts
Correcting Problems	Adapt & Target	Acknowledges criticisms Shows understanding of environment Demonstrates validity of corrective efforts	As above, plus... Corrective efforts done on organization's terms

Because messages spread rapidly, it is important to ensure that: (1) messages are nested under the themes, and (2) messages across themes are not contradictory or leave gaps. Message development should involve some form of 'red-teaming' or murder boards where the messages are subject to critical review – how can the messages be used by opponents against the organization? It may not be possible to mitigate the criticism that could surface, but this exercise would help leaders be proactive and postured to defend the campaign effectively.

---

[151] Original table developed by author.

Table 4. Additional Themes for Transformational Campaigns (Identity Does Change)

Themes of …	Function(s)	Description	Desired Effects
Urgency for Change	Target (Internal)	Presents impetus for change Explains undesired future state Explains risks of insufficient change	Members and Stakeholders aware of need to change & reject status quo
Benefits of Change	Promote	Presents desired future state Presents improved or sustained competitive advantage	As above, plus… Members and Stakeholders accept change effort
Countering Resistance	Target	Addresses arguments to avoid or defer change Addresses risks of lack of priority for change Addresses attempts to interfere with change	As above, plus… Opposition to change muted Change effort supported
Countering Ambivalence	Promote & Defend	Addresses conflicted feelings & anxiety over change Addresses disagreements over the change effort approach Addresses concerns change effort does not go far enough	As above, plus… Change effort understood Discomfort with transition overcome Acceptance of desired future state
Overcoming Cynicism Toward Change	Defend & Target	Counteracts antipathy toward change ("It's going to fail" or "Didn't work before, won't now") Addresses unwarranted withholding of resources and support	Angst over change overcome Change effort supported (or barriers to change removed)

This chapter focused on the actions of the leader and a close-in coalition of members to develop the content of the campaign. It constitutes the first half of the pre-launch phase, essentially setting the communication strategy before translating it into a plan. The presumption is that leaders must have a clear vision of what the named campaign will accomplish before engaging the organization. If leaders do not know what they want, the campaign plan will *not* provide the answer. On the other hand, leaders may not know exactly what they want or may need some flexibility to adapt the campaign vision. Thus, the second half of the pre-launch phase is about setting conditions for launch, which includes targeted socializing of the campaign that provides the leader with the perspectives necessary to refine the vision and provide guidance and direction for planning.

CHAPTER 8. HOW TO LAUNCH A NAMED CAMPAIGN?

WHAT IS *LAUNCH*?

First, let us address the term *launch* and its meaning. When one launches a communication campaign, it is the same as crossing the line of departure. There is no going back. Launch refers to a specific event or series of events that render the campaign active. *Pre-launch* can be characterized as a pre-decisional state, that there is intent to have a campaign but there is room for adjustments, more data and socialization, and the possibility of cancelling altogether with minimal impact on the organization despite the energy devoted to the idea. Launch constitutes commitment to the campaign on the part of the leader and the commitment of resources by the organization.

Oftentimes, leaders conduct the launch publicly and prominently. A big event is held. TV ads air. A new logo is unveiled. Everyone in the unit is called together. But this is not the only way to launch a communication campaign. Launch can occur at a meeting when the senior leader makes the decision to proceed or signs the initiating memorandum. Launch can also occur discreetly, when the leader had made up in the mind that the campaign is underway and behaves accordingly, even though no formal communication has been issued.[152]

Launch is also not necessarily a single event. It can be a 'slow roll-out,' or series of events that expand the reach of the campaign. One can therefore view launch as a phase of synchronized and harmonized activities, all aimed to draw attention to the campaign and announce its beginning.

Regardless of type, launch does not merely happen. It must be properly planned. Big launch events must obviously be planned to carry maximum effect on the target audiences, but so

---

[152] Personal anecdotes from experience. This can happen unintentionally when a busy leader loses track of all the decisions and communications made and believes that enough guidance or intent has been communicated to warrant action by members, who in turn are waiting for precise orders. It can also happen intentionally when the leader feels that the staff is risk-averse or too beholden to formal processes. Thus, the leader conducts a surreptitious launch as a way of judging which members are capable of showing initiative.

too must discreet launches. The leader must know what reactions to expect and how to adapt if audiences react differently. Moreover, the initiation of a change effort does not automatically establish a corresponding communication campaign. The latter supports the former but is separate from it, because the *why* of change in the minds of members and stakeholders may be different from the *why* in the minds of the change effort's champions, and the *who* communicating the why may be different that those involved in the change. Launching a change effort without simultaneously planning the associated communication campaign is unwise.[153]

However, it is always premature to gauge success or failure of the campaign at launch. Rather, it is more appropriate to discuss the performance of the launch. Did the events of the launch reach all the target audiences? Did they respond as anticipated, and was the organization postured to react? The purpose of this chapter is to provide broad guidance on how to approach pre-launch, establish the desired launch events or conditions, and develop measures of performance to determine the near-term effects of the campaign. The chapter is limited on details because there are so many variables to consider and the context of the campaign, preferences of the senior leader, and the strategic environment will not always be predictable in advance. Moreover, organizational communication campaigns are highly subject to the principle of *equifinality*, famously captured by Katz and Kahn in their 1960 book *The Social Psychology of Organizations*. From this principle, "a system can reach the same final state from differing initial conditions and by a variety of paths."[154]

Five Steps to Preparing for Launch

There are five steps to launch preparation and implementation. But note that, as Figure 11 shows, all the work is done *pre-launch*. Although the launch phase will bring along its own requirements for feedback and adjustments, the planning for

---

[153] It also puts the change effort at unnecessary risk of resistance. Several personal experiences involved change efforts (especially experimentation) dictated from higher without any attempt at explaining how the effort will benefit units. Typically, the results were disappointing as members struggled to implement change and resisted at every turn.
[154] Katz and Kahn, 30.

8. LAUNCHING A NAMED CAMPAIGN ❖ 111

acquiring that feedback is done in advance. In practice, the campaign's launch constitutes a complex and carefully controlled activity or sequence of activities. Once the launch starts, it cannot be stopped without putting the organization's narrative at risk. Therefore, planning includes ensuring the most favorable conditions possible for launch.

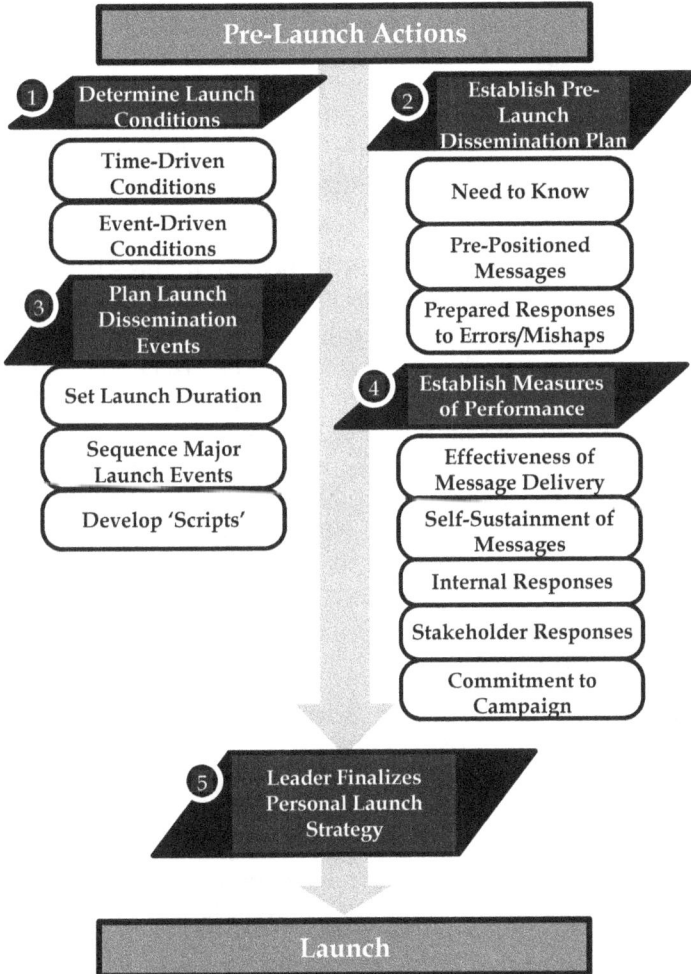

Pre-Launch Actions

1. Determine Launch Conditions
   - Time-Driven Conditions
   - Event-Driven Conditions
3. Plan Launch Dissemination Events
   - Set Launch Duration
   - Sequence Major Launch Events
   - Develop 'Scripts'

2. Establish Pre-Launch Dissemination Plan
   - Need to Know
   - Pre-Positioned Messages
   - Prepared Responses to Errors/Mishaps
4. Establish Measures of Performance
   - Effectiveness of Message Delivery
   - Self-Sustainment of Messages
   - Internal Responses
   - Stakeholder Responses
   - Commitment to Campaign

5. Leader Finalizes Personal Launch Strategy

Launch

Figure 11. Five Steps to Launch a Campaign[155]

---

[155] Original graphic by author.

Step 1. Determine Launch Conditions

The first step is to decide when to launch. While the precise date and time may be dictated in some way—e.g., stakeholder or leader-mandated deadline—that does not necessarily constrain the leader to a specific event at a specific time. In fact, the launch may not have a predetermined date associated with it. The campaign may be best held in a dormant status until conditions are deemed right, so that launch activities provide maximum exposure at the height of audience receptivity. Or, the leader can schedule a disguised launch event – one that makes a public pronouncement of the campaign without actually launching it – to satisfy a stakeholder and buy time to properly plan for the real launch later.[156]

There are two ways to declare launch conditions – *time-driven* or *event-driven*.[157] *Time-driven launches* are set to dates on the calendar, and can be a single date or a period of time bounded with a predetermined start and end. The fixed date can be determined in many ways, but is often tied to an external condition that the organization either does not control or must leverage in order to bring attention to the campaign. At the enterprise level, launches might be based on the fiscal year to leverage the budgetary situation. Sometimes campaigns are time-driven based on the tenure of a senior leader or stakeholder whose departure could negatively affect the campaign. Other times they may be set arbitrarily, such as a leader deadline for action (e.g., "I want X done in 30 days").

Event-driven launches are conditions-based. Once pre-determined desirable conditions have been verified in the environment, launch occurs as soon as practical. Or, if the campaign is the result of a crisis situation, the conditions have essentially already been met and launch must be immediate. There can be greater flexibility in event-driven launches for leaders to delay if the conditions aren't right – for example,

---

[156] Personal anecdote from experience. This tactic has also been used by outgoing leaders under external pressure to 'do' something they do not wish to do, or do not wish to hand over a half-planned communication campaign to a successor who might prefer to go a different direction.

[157] Connie J. G. Gersick, "Pacing Strategic Change: The Case of a New Venture," *Academy of Management Journal* 37, no. 1 (1994): 9-45.

socialization is incomplete, certain barriers to communication are yet unlifted, or the effects of other strategic events are unknown. However, leaders should be concerned about the length of time that passes, as the organization's commitment to the campaign can wither away, rendering the campaign overcome by other activities and forgotten.

Step 2. Establish the Pre-Launch Dissemination Plan

The second step is the *pre-launch* dissemination plan for launch. The purpose of this plan is to determine what types of launch events are required, then preposition information and mobilize the resources necessary to conduct an effective launch. This is like a marketing campaign where the organization must buy all the hats, pens, and brochures with the company's new logo in advance, get them to the storefronts or convention centers, and have marketers standing by having memorized all the messages. While not all communication campaigns require this level of activity, the principles are the same: *Who needs to know what information before launch? Who must NOT know about the campaign now or before launch? Who needs to be prepared at launch to deliver messages - and therefore which messages and to whom? How does the organization respond if news of the campaign is released too soon?*

Again, leaders should not myopically look at the main launch event. They must plan all other activities and communications associated with the launch, such as follow-on press briefings or releases, dissemination through the chain of command, and initial actions of the organization. Leaders will have an easier time planning such activities for time-driven launches. Event-driven launches may require a scaled-down launch using fewer resources that are ready to mobilize quickly.

Pre-launch dissemination planning should allow the organization to exercise a requisite degree of control over the message and organizational activity. However, leaders must assume the possibility of leaks or discovery, or that audiences may successfully guess something about the campaign which might disrupt the desired impact of the launch. Therefore, leaders must anticipate what harm may come of the campaign if prematurely exposed and as best as possible plan for it. On the other hand, some campaigns may benefit from such exposure, called in political terms a *trial balloon*.[158] Leaders may want to test a message in the environment to gauge reaction. If the release proves favorable, leaders may accelerate launch of the campaign or alter the messaging. They can also deny it if the reaction is particularly negative or unexpected, and subsequent avoid such messages in the actual campaign.

Step 3. Plan Launch Dissemination Events

Detailed planning for the dissemination events begins. The organization must set which events go in which sequence and what each event is supposed to accomplish. Sequencing events will depend on the audiences that each event directly engages. For example, if the audience encompasses an entire geographic area of responsibility such as Europe for U.S. European Command or Africa for U.S. Africa Command, there may be a need to engage directly with a multinational body (e.g., Supreme Headquarters Allied Powers Europe or the African Union) before engaging directly with member nations. Or, campaigns involving interagency affairs may require engagement at Cabinet department level before the country teams.

Leaders must also decide how many times to directly engage the same mass audience. Is one 'town hall' at one base or post sufficient? Or must there be multiple engagements scattered at different bases? How many of these engagements will fit in the calendar? To what extent can leaders assume that the preferred message is the one that will spread to individuals not engage? The desired sequencing of launch events may not be feasible due to scheduling and other challenges, but any deviations should be weighed against the risk of some segments of the audience feeling slighted or having been delayed in receiving the organization's messages.

With the events sequenced, the next action is to set the *script* for each event. All launch event provides an opportunity to deliver every message in the campaign, including those audiences not physically present to hear or witness a communication. Scripts

---

[158] Merriam-Webster Online Dictionary, s.v. "Trial Balloon," https://www.merriam-webster.com/dictionary/trial%20balloon (accessed 19 April 2018).

reflect both the messages to disseminate and how to disseminate them. They can be highly prescriptive, such as a speech to be read verbatim. However, such communications can seem inauthentic and off-putting to the receivers. Less prescriptive scripts can be built as 'talking points' or similar construct designed to ensure consistency of the message while allowing flexibility for the speaker.

Red-teaming, or testing and evaluating, the themes and messages will help identify problems with the campaign prior to launch. Planners should assemble a team of members with no direct connection to the campaign's development and/or personnel outside and independent of the organization to evaluate the themes, messages, leader-specific messages, and corporate identity. It is best if the red-team is familiar with the intended audiences of the campaign, stakeholders and third parties alike, especially those with whom the military ordinarily has limited contact such as foreign populations.

Step 4. Establish Measures of Performance

Measures of performance provide the measures for how well the launch phase is executed, under the assumption that high marks will set better conditions for the campaign's success. But as stated earlier in this chapter, leaders must resist the temptation to add measures of effectiveness, in hopes of showing that the campaign is working. Certainly, poor execution at launch can lead to low effectiveness overall. However, the newness of the campaign may create a springboard effect, whereby positive response is inflated and does not necessarily correlate to long-term support for the campaign. A well-executed launch maximizes the potential for garnering member commitment and stakeholder acceptance, but does not guarantee it. A poorly-executed launch engenders resistance, mobilizes opponents, and constrained future actions.

Figure 11 lists suggested measures of performance, many of which will be straightforward. Measures of *effective delivery* relate to the organization's performance in the launch events, along with other organizational activities that coincide. *Did we say what we wanted to say to all those we wanted to say it to?* These are largely negative measures – capturing more of what went wrong rather than what went right. In other words, these measures should address problems in delivery necessitating supplementary action by the organization. Gaps and inconsistencies caused by mistakes, deviations from the script, or planning oversight will all have similar impacts on the campaign, so the organization should concern itself more with adapting the campaign rather than pursuing those who miscommunicated.

Measures of *message self-sustainment* amounts to capturing the immediate say-hear gaps among receivers. Are there indications that the audience misheard the message? Is the mishearing the result of confusion, conflation of terms, or latent biases? Although acceptance of the message is always desired, at launch it is more important to ensure that the direct receivers heard the message right.

Measures of *internal response* are those related to how much the organization is demonstrating commitment to its own campaign. Are members doing the minimal necessary according to the launch event plan or are they showing receptivity and ownership of the campaign? Resistance and ambivalence toward the campaign will likely continue, however leaders should expect a change in its character once launch occurs and resistance to the campaign's existence is futile. Will resistance become ambivalence as opponents cease getting in the way? Or, will is change to support as leader commitment to the campaign is demonstrated in the launch?

Stakeholder response is very important, and they may be the first to show indications that the campaign is having an effect. Of course, any negative or ambivalent reaction may lead to later decisions to withhold support or resources.

Step 5. Finalize Leader's Personal Communication Strategy

Through the process, leaders evaluate their personal roles in the launch and how their activities will be harmonized with the organization's efforts. Leaders should communicate with their staffs and leadership teams how they will approach deciding that the conditions for launch are met. Will it be through a formal communication stating that the campaign has begun or informally by exception (e.g., the campaign launches unless the commander explicitly stops it). Similarly, leaders must set clear expectations on the extent to which they must be informed about the dissemination plan. Under what circumstances must the leader be informed about and make decisions about the launch based on premature release of information or extenuating circumstances potentially impeding the launch?

The most challenging aspect for the leader is choosing which launch events to actively participate in, which to observe, which to delegate to others on the leadership team to oversee, and which to maintain a low leadership profile. Without question, those that the leader personally attend will receive greater attention, and the audiences may notice the differences (e.g., that audience got the commander while only the deputy came to visit us). Leaders may use multimedia as a means of expanding one's personal profile over the campaign, such as social media releases and recorded messages to be delivered at launch events. Decisions on levels of participation also rest on other demands of the leader.

Leaders also have to weigh risks associated with their choices. The levels of participation can have an effect on post-launch expectations. A leader who is everywhere promoting the launch early on will likely not be able to sustain that tempo afterward, which may prompt opponents to suggest the campaign is a flash in the pan. A leader misstep could have a greater impact on the campaign than a misstep by a member. Also, opponents may choose to target the leader with criticisms unrelated to the campaign and thus interrupt the desired momentum.

One thing leaders should avoid is being their own judges regarding the measures of performance. The leader's perspective could be unduly rosy or be overly self-critical. It is difficult for leaders to be objective over their own performance at launch events, thus it is important to rely on independent or unbiased sources.

CHAPTER 9. HOW TO SUSTAIN AND END NAMED CAMPAIGNS?

Ok, you have successfully launched the campaign. *What now?*

Obviously, post-launch is not the time to ask this question! This point cannot be stressed enough, sustainment of the campaign has to be planned (albeit with a lot of flexibility) from the beginning. Leaders should have already built a mental picture of how the desired outcomes will be achieved, because inevitably something is going to go 'wrong' – there will be missteps by the organization, and adversaries will mobilize and launch opposing messages. It is to be expected, and it takes a well-planned campaign built for the long-term to overcome it.

Just as importantly, however, is that the campaign must not go on beyond its usefulness. Messages can go stale or the situation changes. The leader must be willing and able to adjust or terminate a campaign that is not bring about the desired effects. *How does this campaign end* is as important as getting the campaign going.

WHAT IS POST-LAUNCH PLANNING?

This final chapter is about post-launch planning during pre-launch. It need not be detailed to the same extent. Yet, it involves establishing the measures of effectiveness and key data indicators so that the organization can detect what lasting effects the campaign is having on the environment. Planning during post-launch sets the 'battle rhythm' of the campaign after the initial attention to it has faded. How much effort will the organization put into the campaign during the first, second, third year and so on? How will the organization determine when the campaign should end?

Before getting into the activities, this Step begins with an explanation of two dangers facing campaigns at post-launch – *complacency* and *myopia*. Both can result in the loss of member or stakeholder commitment and the resurgence of opposition to the organization. Post-launch is about keeping the campaign strong while keeping these dangers in check.

Complacency is the emerging lack of will to communicate the messages of the campaign. Leaders, members, stakeholders, or others determine that other communications have priority or have lost interest in further the campaign's messages. Sometimes, this is because the campaign is doing 'well,' meaning that the campaign is meeting its targets in measures of performance and the members do not feel it necessary to continue to expend energy toward the campaign. Sometimes, this is a result of the campaign flagging during launch, and members might prefer not to be associated with a failed effort. Other times, it is a matter of individual resistance or ambivalence to the campaign, leading to message fatigue and disinterest. Complacency can both kill the campaign and undo any positive effects that came from it.

Myopia is even more damaging than complacency because organizations can believe they are sustaining a viable campaign when there are instead weakening it. Myopia is defined as "a lack of foresight" and "a narrow view of something."[159] The onset of myopia is often post-launch, when the organization reduces the energy it expends on the campaign and thus reduces its scope and intensity to make room for other priorities. This narrowing of scope can become a pattern as other activities impinge further into the campaign. Overcoming myopia involves a combination of leader and member self-awareness, a willingness to explore disconfirming data and challenge assumptions, and a suitable and acceptable injection of new messages into the campaign.

FIVE STEPS TO POST-LAUNCH PLANNING

Figure 12 depicts the five Steps in post-launch planning prior to launch. The overall approach is focusing on the durable elements. For example, when determining the measures of effectiveness, it is best to identify measures from which one should be able to collect the same type of data on today, next month, and years from now. One should not choose measures whose meaning may change or for whom different data sources may be required in the future, as this will lead to apples-and-oranges comparisons. Inevitably, the natural changes in the environment will complicate measuring success, so flexibility is

---

[159] https://www.merriam-webster.com/dictionary/myopia

key, but it is more important to keep the initial post-launch plan as simple as possible.

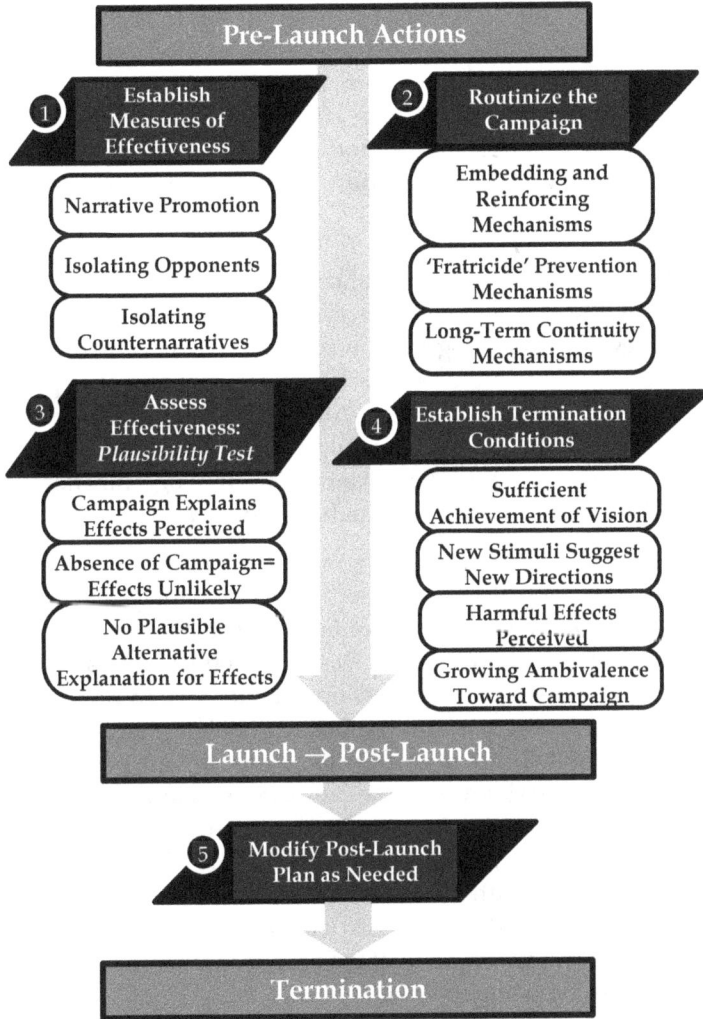

Pre-Launch Actions

1. Establish Measures of Effectiveness
   - Narrative Promotion
   - Isolating Opponents
   - Isolating Counternarratives

2. Routinize the Campaign
   - Embedding and Reinforcing Mechanisms
   - 'Fratricide' Prevention Mechanisms
   - Long-Term Continuity Mechanisms

3. Assess Effectiveness: *Plausibility Test*
   - Campaign Explains Effects Perceived
   - Absence of Campaign= Effects Unlikely
   - No Plausible Alternative Explanation for Effects

4. Establish Termination Conditions
   - Sufficient Achievement of Vision
   - New Stimuli Suggest New Directions
   - Harmful Effects Perceived
   - Growing Ambivalence Toward Campaign

Launch → Post-Launch

5. Modify Post-Launch Plan as Needed

Termination

Figure 12. Post-Launch and Termination[160]

---

[160] Original graphic by author.

Step 1. Establish Measures of Effectiveness

The first activity for campaign sustainment relates to the organization's interface with the external environment. It had already described the campaign vision as an environment with the organization's narrative promoted and adversaries and their messages isolated. None of these effects occur during the launch phase as they require time and reinforcement through the organization's words and actions. They will only come about during post-launch.

Planners want to define quantitatively or qualitatively what factors in the environment *perceptible by the organization* can provide evidence of progress toward vision achievement. From this, the organization places *sensors* in the environment to gather evidence and perform analysis. Although specific guidance on choosing sensors is beyond the scope of this book, these sensors can be human (internal or external to the organization) or automated depending on the data being collected.

The quickest way to identify measures of effectiveness is to look at the three main outcomes of named campaigns. The first regards *narrative promotion*. Named campaigns enhance the standing campaign. Therefore, measures of effectiveness indicate the extent to which the organization is better able to promote its narrative as a result of the named campaign. The following questions may help identify possible measures for post-launch: (1) How do leaders know that the campaign's vision is making the needed changes to the organization's identity, its competitive advantage, its image, or its reputation? (2) How do leaders know that relationships with other audiences, especially stakeholders, is changing as desired? (3) How do leaders know that these effects are enduring and that the end of the named campaign will not see progress quickly being undone?

The second category of measure regards how leaders would know that the campaign's or organization's *opponents are becoming isolated*, at least in a relative sense. The opponent may continue to communicate, but what indicators may show that their influence is waning? Maybe there are indicators that stakeholders are no longer responding to their messages and therefore putting less pressure on the organization. Perhaps the measure can determine if they are given less credence by the public at large, or that their circles of contacts are becoming tighter such that they only communicate with like-minded audiences.

The last category measures *counternarrative isolation*. Similar to the above, the measures should indicate that other audiences are unwilling to share opposing messages because ostensibly they question their veracity on the basis of the named campaign.

Step 2. Routinize the Campaign

Routinizing refers to the appropriate incorporation of the campaign in the routine activities of the organization. It does not imply making the campaign so 'routine' that it ceases to impart meaning. Rather, it means that the institutional practices within the organization are given authorities, responsibilities, and duties to sustain the campaign over the long term. This potentially involves adjustments to each of the three pillars of institutional practice – formal, informal, and related to shared understandings among the membership. Routinizing in the formal sense is easy – one can always dictate yet another meeting or reporting requirement -- but it is not necessarily effect.

Routinizing the campaign has three main components. First is identifying *embedding and reinforcing mechanisms*[161] for the campaign. Embedding mechanisms help anchor the campaign in the organization, helping it to communicate with the campaign in mind. Reinforcing mechanisms help sustain the campaign in institutional memory over time. While other competing activities may divert energy away, the reinforcing mechanisms should permit the restoration of such energy as desired.

The second part is setting *fratricide prevention mechanisms*.[162] Put another way, how does the campaign prevent itself from negatively impacting other campaigns? How do prioritization and messaging across campaigns remain synchronized? What are red flags that the organization should look out for? Obviously,

---

[161] Schein, *Organizational Culture*, 235-236.

[162] I am drawing from the metaphor of *communication fratricide* in terms of friendly communications jamming each other due to poor frequency management. For example, see Brian S. Filibeck and Corey M. Swetz, "Achieving Spectrum Dominance in the Combat Aviation Brigade," *Aviation Digest 1*, no. 2 (April-June 2013): 35-37.

one cannot always avoid contradiction across the many active campaigns of the organization, but at a minimum the members should be aware of how the present campaign overlaps with or relates to other named campaigns of the organization, and the campaigns that stakeholders may be implementing.

Finally, there is the *long-term continuity mechanisms*. Turnover in military organizations means constant re-learning and re-training in the campaign. How is information about the campaign transferred from outgoing personnel to incoming? Or what is the indoctrination plan for new personnel? What about special considerations for the leaders who will steward the narrative and govern the communication process?[163]

Step 3. Identify the Parameters for the "Plausibility Test" of Success

Attributing the effects causally to the campaign is difficult, if not impossible. The natural complexity of the communication environment provides opportunities for many possible explanations for any long-term beneficial outcomes. In short, leaders must not overdetermine the campaign's success. If there is convincing evidence to show that a desired outcome was caused by something other than the campaign, leaders should be truthful and acknowledge it but that evidence is also likely unconvincing.

While data collection on the campaign's effects is important and necessary, leaders cannot rely on deterministic or scientific approaches to verify the campaign's impact. In another words, the sum of favorable assessments of the measures of effectiveness will rarely equal achievement of the overall campaign vision. Instead, leaders must rely on their judgment to determine to what extent the campaign influenced the environment favorable to the organization. The operative question follows: *is it plausible that the campaign brought about the perceived effects in the environment?*

---

[163] The challenges of joining communication campaigns in the middle of implementation mirror those of on-going change efforts. This is discussed at length in Thomas P. Galvin, *Driving Change: A Primer for Senior Leaders* (Carlisle, PA: Department of Command, Leadership, and Management, in press).

I call this the *plausibility test*,[164] and has three components: (1) does the presence of the campaign explain the effects perceived, (2) does the absence of the campaign means that the effects would likely not have been perceived, and (3) no other actor in the environment could have produced the effects? The plausibility test seeks the most likely explanation for the effects rather than scientifically deriving an unequivocal deterministic cause. The important idea is to avoid claiming success on coincidence alone, there has to be a demonstrable connection between the campaign and the effects that a reasonable disinterested party could accept. The lack of scientific proof means that not all audiences will accept the organization's judgment – and opponents are equally likely to either disagree with the effects perceived or argue against the effects being the result of the organization's action.

The parameters for the "plausibility test" for effectiveness constitute a bullet list or prose statement of key indicators that the campaign is achieving overall success – possibly commensurate with and possible in spite of the measures of effectiveness previously identified. Consider the following questions when putting together this test.

1. How will one determine whether the overall positive effects seen in the environment can plausibly be attributed to the campaign? In other words, identify component parts of the vision that are most likely to occur as a result of the campaign. Then, connect those with the campaign's measures of effectiveness – such that the better the measure the more likely the campaign vision will be realized.

2. What parts of the vision are presently not adequately covered by a measure of effectiveness? If it is something unmeasurable, then is there a way to

---

164 This is loosely based on *plausibility reasoning* used in ancient times to aid in rendering judgments in court cases when there were no eyewitnesses. Manfred Kraus, "Early Greek Probability Arguments and Common Ground in Dissensus," *OSSA Conference Archive* 92 (2007), https://scholar.uwindsor.ca/cgi/viewcontent.cgi?referer=https://en.wikipedia.org/&https redir=1&article=1344&context=ossaarchive (accessed 19 April 2018).

gauge how the campaign's success constitutes the most likely explanation for vision achievement?

3. Reviewing the above, consider the following: If the campaign were not to occur, how likely is it that the vision would <u>not</u> possibly be achieved? In essence, this is the converse of causality – we might be challenged to prove that campaign achieved an effect but we may have an easier time determining that the absence of the campaign would have ensured a much lesser result.

Step 4. Set Termination Conditions for the Campaign

When does the campaign end? Or more importantly, how? Does it fade to black as its effects are realized but before the campaign's benefits no longer exceed its costs? Does it end abruptly, celebrated at sets off gloriously to the setting sun or cursed as is it cancelled? Is vision achievement really the end state or is it instead a new beginning to some further goal? Planning ahead for the campaign's termination is not planning for failure! Rather, it is important to recognize in advantage those signs and signals that say the campaign is failing or has reached the limits of its effects without further modification.

Termination conditions represent a special case of measures of effectiveness. Some may derive from the failure to achieve desired effects, while others are effects of the campaign that are not anticipated and not desired. A campaign to win 'hearts and minds,' for example, might completely backfire and stir up anti-American sentiment. If such sentiment appears, leaders face a decision whether it is better to pull the plug on the campaign before further damage occurs.

The following questions may help in identifying termination conditions of the campaign. These will necessarily be broad and may be refined during the campaign's implementation. Leaders may also establish mitigation strategies:

(1) Which established measures of effectiveness (Step 1 of this Chapter) would, if the effects were negative, signal the need to possibly terminate the campaign?

(2) What about cost-benefit ratios, in which the energy expended toward the measures was too great for the benefits achieved?

(3) What about the ability to sustain the organization's energy levels? If the organization were distracted by another priority or crisis, how much reversal of the campaign's effect would be tolerated before a decision to terminate?

(4) What are conditions that signal the organization's lack of interest or ambivalence toward the campaign, such that injecting further leader emphasis or energy would do more harm than good?

(5) Are there signs of fratricide with other campaigns to look out for?

(6) What is the 'good enough' point that the campaign has achieved adequate effects and it is better to launch a new or different campaign rather than continue the current?

Build the termination assessment plan. The purpose is to identify appropriate venues for considering the continuance or termination of the campaign without placing the campaign on the constant defensive. That is, if one were to ask too often about possibly ending the campaign, it may bias the organization in favor of ending it prematurely. Instead, consider the following as natural decision points that leaders can leverage, or come up with your own.

Step 5. Modify Post-Launch Plan as Needed

To follow the old adage, no plan survives first contact with the enemy. This final step in post-launch planning occurs from the time that launch approaches through completion of launch activities and commensurate assessment of launch performance. It is during this period that the challenges of the change efforts implementation will be clearer and one can baseline where the organization was at launch. This way, leaders can strive to segregate the actual effects of the change effort over time from other factors – such as collateral damage (or collateral assistance) from other change efforts or changes in the environment.

Do the measures hold up, and are they as measurable as assumed during planning? One should not wait very long after launch to begin attempts at collecting the data and assessing its reliability. It is easy to adjust the measures at launch than realize later on that the wrong measures were identified. The further from launch the effort progresses the harder it will be to adjust measures because the dynamics of the environment will influence them over time.

Routinization is another time-sensitive matter. Post-launch success is enhanced when launch spurs internal action to change habits and think differently. Put the planned new routines into action quickly using the planned embedding mechanisms and institute the reinforcing mechanisms sooner rather than later if possible. Otherwise, the organization down the road will treat such changes of routine as new, unnecessary disruptions.

It is very hard to overcommunicate change,[165] unless it is the same message repeating itself constantly. Messaging throughout the post-launch phase must be fresh and relevant. John Kotter talks about capturing short-term wins, a suitable approach. Celebrating successes, especially in action, is important for keeping the campaign's momentum. But the celebration should have meaning to show that the good words and deeds are springboards to better things – a better performing organization, a healthier reputation, or the capitulation of an adversary. On the other hand, punishments and sanctions communicate volumes as well, especially if they appear to negate the campaign's goals. Consistent messaging is hard, especially in complex organizations, so leaders must intensely monitor the environment and the membership to detect and respond to gaps and inconsistencies that almost inevitably arise in any communication campaign.

---

165 Kotter, *Leading Change*, 94-95.

CONCLUSION

This Primer covers an incredible amount of ground, because communication campaigns are complicated and difficult to establish. As shown in the introduction, there are many shortcuts that leaders like to take – come up with a pithy slogan or cool logo, toss some video and audio behind it, and zap! Hearts and minds are changed. Unlike most other organizational phenomena, communication is still largely treated as though leaders have a disproportionate level of control. Charisma and oratory skill will save the day! This could not be further from the truth.

The U.S. defense enterprise comprises two million people. Indeed, its senior civilian and military leaders carry considerable weight when they speak and act. The Chief of Staff of the Army's annual address at the annual Association of the U.S. Army convention shows that service members put a lot of stock in leader communications. But such actions represent only a single event in an overall Army-wide effort to promote its narrative, an effort that is as continuous as it is difficult. From Department of Defense, joint, and service levels down to the company, platoon, and small-unit teams, it is the same truth – leaders have their role to play to personally communicate, but it takes the whole team to turn the leader's intentions into the desired effects. There are no shortcuts.

The purpose of this Primer was to provide a roadmap for understanding both where the organization is – the *standing campaign* – and how to intervene in it – the *named campaign*. Although the Primer goes into considerable detail as to what these campaigns are and how to build them, much of the work in campaigns I have been involved in were accomplished through quality collaboration and common sense. Naturally, if the members do not understand their organization's story well, someone must convey it to them, and putting that story together is not easily done if there is a wealth of history to wade through. This process takes a lot of time because it requires depth. Pithy slogans and cool logos may draw attention, but they ultimately explain very little.

There are also no shortcuts in execution. They fool no one and embolden adversaries who will use their 15-to-1 asymmetric advantage to hammer the organization and its leaders. Why? Because they can. It is as simple as that. Organizations that do not communicate, who take a risk averse approach to engagement, are just as vulnerable. The winners in this environment are those who speak and act consistently, with purpose, and continuously. No leader can do this alone – it is a team effort, which means that the whole team must be in on the campaign. This can be especially difficult in organizations that are diverse, such as in the joint, interagency, intergovernmental, or multinational arenas.

But it can be done. Success is possible, and has been demonstrated. The U.S. Africa Command establishment is a prominent example, an effort that successfully turned a hostile environment into a mostly supportive one. The campaign tooks months to form and it required a lot of effort to synchronize and harmonize activities all the way up and down the chain. But it was done, and many of the lessons of that campaign inspired the questions and methods built into this Primer.

This Primer is imperfect almost by nature. Ways and means of communicating evolve over time, so I welcome your counsel regarding its contents. The goal was to provide a *how-to* guide to give leaders a headstart, but its suggestions may not work for every organization in every circumstance. I welcome your feedback, and I wish you success in whatever communication campaign you resolve to implement in your organization.

TO LEARN MORE

Albert, Stuart and David A. Whetten, "Organizational Identity," *Research in Organizational Behavior* 7 (1985): 263-295.

Balmer, John M., Kyoko Fukukawa, and Edmund R. Gray, "The Nature and Management of Ethical Corporate Identity: A Commentary on Corporate Identity, Corporate Social Responsibility, and Ethics," *Journal of Business Ethics* 76, no. 1 (November 2007): 7-15.

Bamberg, Michael and Molly Andrews (Eds.), *Considering Counter-Narratives: Narrating, Resisting, Making Sense* (Amsterdam: John Benjamins, 2004).

Bolt, Neville, "Strategic Communications in Crisis," *RUSI Journal* 156, no. 4 (2011): 44-53.

Clarkson, Max B. E., "A Stakeholder Framework for Analyzing and Evaluating Corporate Social Performance," *The Academy of Management Review* 20, no. 1 (Janaury 1995): 92-117.

Cornish, Paul, Julian Lindley-French, and Claire Yorke, *Strategic Communications and National Strategy* (London: Chatham House, Royal Institute of International Affairs, 2011).

Department of Defense, *Report of the Defense Science Board: Task Force on Strategic Communication* (Washington, DC: Department of Defense, 2009).

Dutton, Jane E. and Janet M. Dukerich, "Keeping an Eye on the Mirror: Image and Identity in Organizational Adaptation," *The Academy of Management Journal* 34, no. 3 (September 1991), 517-554.

Eder, Mari K., *Leading the Narrative: The Case for Strategic Communication* (Annapolis, MD: Naval Institute Press, 2011).

Galvin, Thomas P., *Two Case Studies of Successful Communication Campaigns* (Carlisle, PA: U.S. Army War College Press, in press).

Gibbons, Paul, *The Science of Successful Organizational Change* (New York: Pearson, 2015).

Gibb, Jack R., "Defensive Communication," *Journal of Communication* 11, no. 3, (September 1961): 141-148.

Gioia, Dennis A., Majken Schultz, and Kevin G. Corley, "Organizational identity, image, and adaptive instability." *Academy of Management Review* 25, no. 1 (2000): 63-81.

Halloran, Richard, "Strategic Communication," *Parameters* 37, No. 3 (Autumn 2007): 4-14.

Kotter, John, *Leading Change* (Boston, MA: Harvard University Press, 1996).

Lange, Donald, Peggy M. Lee, and Ye Dai. "Organizational Reputation: A Review." *Journal of Management* 37, no. 1 (2011): 153-184.

McQuail, Denis, *Mass Communication Theory: An Introduction* (London: Sage, 1983).

Mintzberg, Henry, *The Nature of Managerial Work* (Englewood Cliffs, NJ: Prentice-Hall, 1973).

Mitchell, Ronald K., Bradley R. Agle, and Donna J. Wood, "Toward a Theory of Stakeholder Identification and Salience: Defining the Principle of Who and What Really Counts," *The Academy of Management Review* 22, no. 4 (October 1997): 853-886.

Oliver, Christine, "The Antecedents of Deinstitutionalization," *Organization Studies* 13, no. 4 (1992): 563-588, 567.

Schein, Edgar H., *Organizational Culture and Leadership*, 4th Edition (San Francisco: Jossey-Bass, 2010).

Scott, W. Richard, *Institutions and Organizations* (Thousand Oaks, CA: Sage, 2008).

Stamp, Glen H., Anita L. Vangelisti, and John A. Daly, "The Creation of Defensiveness in Social Interaction," *Communication Quarterly* 40, no. 2 (1992): 177-190.

Tatham, Steven, *U.S. Governmental Information Operations and Strategic Communications: A Discredited Tool or User Failure? Implications for Future Conflict* (Carlisle, PA: Strategic Studies Institute, 2013).

U.S. Department of the Army, *Mission Command*, Army Doctrinal Reference Publication 6-0 (Washington, DC: U.S. Department of the Army, 2012).

U.S. Joint Forces Command, *Commander's Handbook for Strategic Communication and Communication Strategy*, Version 3.0 (Norfolk, VA: Joint

Whetten, David A., "Albert and Whetten Revisited: Strengthening the Concept of Organizational Identity," *Journal of Management Inquiry* 15, no. 3 (September 2006): 219-234.

Whetten, David A. and Paul C. Godfrey (Eds.), *Identity in Organizations: Building Theory Through Conversations* (Thousand Oaks, CA: Sage, 1998).

THE UNITED STATES ARMY WAR COLLEGE

The United States Army War College educates and develops leaders for service at the strategic level while advancing knowledge in the global application of Landpower.

The purpose of the United States Army War College is to produce graduates who are skilled critical thinkers and complex problem solvers. Concurrently, it is our duty to the U.S. Army to also act as a "think factory" for commanders and civilian leaders at the strategic level worldwide and routinely engage in discourse and debate concerning the role of ground forces in achieving national security objectives.

The Strategic Studies Institute publishes national security and strategic research and analysis to influence policy debate and bridge the gap between military and academia.

The Center for Strategic Leadership contributes to the education of world class senior leaders, develops expert knowledge, and provides solutions to strategic Army issues affecting the national security community.

The Peacekeeping and Stability Operations Institute provides subject matter expertise, technical review, and writing expertise to agencies that develop stability operations concepts and doctrines.

The School of Strategic Landpower develops strategic leaders by providing a strong foundation of wisdom grounded in mastery of the profession of arms, and by serving as a crucible for educating future leaders in the analysis, evaluation, and refinement of professional expertise in war, strategy, operations, national security, resource management, and responsible command.

The U.S. Army Heritage and Education Center acquires, conserves, and exhibits historical materials for use to support the U.S. Army, educate an international audience, and honor Soldiers—past and present.

www.ingramcontent.com/pod-product-compliance
Lightning Source LLC
Chambersburg PA
CBHW081416270326
41931CB00015B/3293